'This original collection of international studies brings together a range of theoretical perspectives to show how children's literature can be effectively used in the multilingual classroom. The book will inspire researchers, teachers and educators around the world who are seeking ways to draw upon and foster children's linguistic and cultural resources.'

Dr Charmian Kenner, Goldsmiths, University of London

'This is an inspirational book revealing the cognitive, social and emotional strengths of migrant children when teachers promote the home languages and stories of their families. It illustrates innovative and excellent pedagogical practice by teachers across the world and thus provides an essential resource for classrooms and teacher education courses.'

Professor Eve Gregory, Goldsmiths, University of London

D0761522

Children's Literature in Multilingual Classrooms

IOEPress Trentham Books

This book is dedicated to
Nil, Luan, Sophie, Charlotte, Alex and Helen,
the children and grandchildren born to the
authors during this book's production.

Children's Literature in Multilingual Classrooms

From multiliteracy to multimodality

Edited by Christine Hélot, Raymonde Sneddon and Nicola Daly

Foreword by Jim Cummins

A Trentham Book
Institute of Education Press

First published in 2014 by the Institute of Education, University of London,
20 Bedford Way, London WC1H 0AL
www.ioe.ac.uk/ioepress

British Library Cataloguing in Publication Data:
A catalogue record for this publication is available from the British Library

ISBNs
978-1-85856-557-6 (paperback)
978-1-85856-648-1 (PDF eBook)
978-1-85856-649-8 (ePub eBook)
978-1-85856-650-4 (Kindle eBook)

Typeset by Quadrant Infotech (India) Pvt Ltd
Printed by CPI Group (UK) Ltd, Croydon CR0 4YY
Cover art: Ayshat Gukhaeva / MariaTkach (Thinkstock)

Contents

Acknowledgements

Our grateful thanks to the many teachers and students who have shared their questions with us and challenged us to think critically about literacy and multilingualism.

About the contributors

Nicola Daly is Senior Lecturer in the Faculty of Education, University of Waikato, New Zealand. Her background is in sociolinguistics (Victoria University of Wellington, New Zealand) and Human Communication Sciences (La Trobe University, Australia). She is currently responsible for language teacher education with preservice teachers and for a compulsory course in culturally responsive pedagogy at the University of Waikato. Her interest in and passion for picture books has been lifelong, and she has happily been able to incorporate this passion into her research, examining the use of Māori loanwords in New Zealand English picture books; the use of picture books in diverse New Zealand classrooms; and, most recently, the use of picture books in teacher education. She has recent publications in *Bookbird* and the *Journal of Children's Literature Studies*. nicolad@waikato.ac.nz

Maria González Davies is Associate Professor at the Modern Languages Department of the Faculty of Education (FPCEE), Ramon Llull University in Barcelona, Spain. She has taught English in primary schools and at the University of Barcelona as well as translation and children's literature at the Universities of Barcelona and of Vic, where she was Head of the Translation Department. She has also published research on translation, foreign language learning and on children's and young adults' literature. Her publications include *Whose Story? Translating the verbal and the visual in literature for young readers* (Cambridge Scholars Publishing, 2009), co-edited with Riitta Oittinen, and *New Trends in Early Foreign Language Learning: Bridging research and good practices regarding the use of the L1, translation, CLIL and the age factor*, co-edited with Annarita Taronna (Cambridge Scholars Publishing, 2012). She is also the co-author of *Exploring Translation: Language in action* with Richard Samson (Routledge, 2014). mariagd@blanquerna.url.edu

Christine Hélot has been Professor of English in the Teacher Education Department of the University of Strasbourg (France) since 1991. From 1975 to 1990, she held a post as Lecturer in Applied Linguistics at the National University of Ireland (Maynooth College) where she was the director of the Language Centre. As a sociolinguist, her research focuses on language in education policies in France and in Europe, bi-multilingual education, intercultural education, early childhood education, and children's literature and multiliteracy.

In 1988 she obtained her PhD from Trinity College (Dublin, Ireland) for a thesis entitled *Child Bilingualism: A linguistic and sociolinguistic study*, and in 2005 she was awarded an *Habilitation* by the University of Strasbourg for her research on bilingualism in the home and school contexts. This research was published in French in 2007 by l'Harmattan (Paris) under the title *Du Bilinguisme en famille au plurilinguisme à l'école*. Since 2009, Dr Hélot has been a regular participant in the Master's in Bilingual Education run by Pablo de Olavide University (Seville, Spain). During 2011/12, she was a guest professor at the Goethe University of Frankfurt am Main (Germany) in the Institute for Romance Languages and Literatures. She has published widely in French and English.
christine.helot@gmail.com

Heather Lotherington is Professor of Multilingual Education at York University in Toronto where she teaches in the Faculty of Education, and in the Graduate Program in Linguistics and Applied Linguistics. She has taught Applied Linguistics, Sociolinguistics, Language and Literacy Education, TESL and Research Methodology at universities in Canada, Australia, Fiji, Germany and England. Her research interests focus on multimodality; multilingual and plurilingual education; language, literacy and technology; and pedagogical innovation in the digital age. She spearheaded a decade-long, award-winning collaborative research venture between York University and Joyce Public School (Toronto District School Board), bringing together researchers and teachers to co-develop multimodal literacies pedagogies in project-based learning (see www.multiliteracies4kidz.ca). Their tangible successes in designing a sustainable model of innovative classroom teaching, learning and internal professional development inspired her current research into the recurring gaps in academic and social conceptions of communication across the complex educational infrastructure. She is now working with an international team to systematically investigate how communicative competence can be revised for the digital age. Professor Lotherington's most recent book is *Pedagogy of Multiliteracies: Rewriting Goldilocks* (Routledge, 2011).
HLotherington@edu.yorku.ca

Roy Lyster is Professor of Second Language Education in the Department of Integrated Studies in Education at McGill University in Canada. He has a PhD in Applied Linguistics as well as a BEd and MEd from the University of Toronto, and an MA from the Université de Paris VII. His research examines content-based second language instruction and the effects of instructional interventions designed to counterbalance form-focused and content-based approaches. His research interests also include the professional development of immersion teachers as well as teacher collaboration across the curriculum. His research has been published in journals such as *Studies in Second Language Acquisition, Language Learning, Language Teaching Research, Language Awareness, Applied Linguistics, Journal of Immersion and Content-Based Education* and *The Modern Language Journal*. He was co-president then president of the Canadian Association of Applied Linguistics from 2004 to 2008 and serves on the Advisory Committees of *Studies in Second Language Acquisition* and *The Canadian Modern Language Review*, and on the Editorial Boards of *Language Teaching Research* and the *Journal of Immersion and Content-Based Education*. He is author of *Learning and Teaching Languages Through Content: A counterbalanced approach*, published by Benjamins in 2007. roy.lyster@mcgill.ca

Judith Oller completed her PhD in Psychology in 2008. She is an Associate Teacher at the University of Girona and also a Consultant in Education and Psychology at the Open University of Catalonia (UOC). With the aims of promoting immigrant students' academic performance and helping teachers to develop cross-cultural literacy and awareness, she has been involved in research related to bilingual education, critical multiliteracies and teachers' preparation. Her research interests relate to three complementary fields: second language acquisition in multilingual contexts, inclusive education and the development of communitarian research-action programmes to link home and school literacy practices and foster the participation of minority groups in society. She is currently involved in two projects (one in Catalonia and the other in Mexico) to recover oral traditional fairy tales of minority groups and to create bilingual material through the use of a multiliteracies approach. Some of her publications can be accessed from the following web page: https://sites.google.com/site/judithollerbadenas/publications. Judith.oller@udg.edu

Stefan Pernes is a recent graduate of the Applied Linguistics Master's programme at the University of Vienna. His thesis evolved around the M2 multiclass and the Little Books' writing culture that is also covered in the present volume. During his studies he focused on methodology and multimodality. His work experience includes arts management, software development and early childhood education.
stefan.pernes@gmail.com

Sari Pietikäinen is Professor of Discourse Studies at the Department of Languages, University of Jyväskylä, Finland. Working within the fields of applied linguistics, discourse studies and media studies, her research interests include changing multilingualisms, the indigenous Sámi community and shifting boundaries between languages and their users. Among her recent publications are *Multilingualism and the Periphery* (Oxford University Press, 2013), edited together with Helen Kelly-Holmes, and 'Multilingual dynamics in Sámiland: A rhizomatic discourse approach to changing language' (in *International Journal of Bilingualism,* 2013). Address for correspondence: Department of Languages, PO Box 35, FIN-40014 University of Jyväskylä, Finland.
sari.p.pietikainen@jyu.fi

Anne Pitkänen-Huhta, PhD, is Senior Lecturer in English at the Department of Languages, University of Jyväskylä, Finland, and Head of the Department of Languages. She has also worked as a senior researcher and domain coordinator in the Centre of Excellence for the Study of Variation, Contacts and Change in English (2006–12, funded by the Academy of Finland, director Professor Terttu Nevalainen) and as a temporary professor of English, language learning and teaching (2007–13) at the Department of Languages, University of Jyväskylä. Her research focuses on multilingual literacy and discourse practices, especially of young people, on foreign language learning in formal and informal contexts and on the role of English in Finnish society. Her research employs ethnographic and discourse analytic as well as survey methods. She is the editor of *Literacy Practices in Transition: Perspectives from the Nordic countries*(Multilingual Matters, 2012) together with Lars Holm.

Address for correspondence: Department of Languages, PO Box 35, FIN-40014 University of Jyväskylä, Finland.
anne.pitkanen-huhta@jyu.fi

Christian Schreger is a teacher at the Ortnergasse Primary School in Vienna. He is a co-initiator of the 'Viennese Modern School Multiclasses' school pilot project (1997) and runs his own multiclass 'M2'. He has been actively participating in the Freinet movement and is now a teacher educator, holding seminars at the University of Teacher Education in Vienna, among other places, and publishing in various journals. His projects receive awards relating to themes such as children and the internet, the inclusion and advancement of children of immigrants and minorities, and the integration of multilingualism in the classroom. Notable examples include the state-award-winning 'WeltABC', a multimodal and multilingual online lexicon organized by children themselves, and the haptic 'Little Books' project where children take the role of authors, using a variety of tools.
post@weltabc.at

Raymonde Sneddon is Research Fellow in Language and Education at the Cass School of Education and Communities, University of East London (UEL). Her PhD is in Applied Linguistics from Birkbeck College, University of London. She was a primary teacher in east London for 17 years specializing in working with bilingual pupils, their families and communities. She has been making dual language books with children and their families since the early 1980s. Until 2004 she was a teacher educator at UEL and was involved with national projects to develop teachers' understanding of the educational needs of bilingual pupils. Her research interests are in the field of multilingualism and multiliteracy, community language teaching and complementary education. Her book *Bilingual Books – Biliterate Children: Learning to read with dual language books* was published by Trentham Books in 2009. Recent papers include 'Telling the story of the Computer Geek: Children becoming authors and translators' (*Language and Education*, 2012) and 'Alternative spaces of learning in east London: Opportunities and challenges' (with Peter Martin, 2012). Address for correspondence: Cass School of Education and Communities, UEL, Water Lane, Stratford, London E15 4LZ.
Raymonde.sneddon@zen.co.uk

Caterina Sugranyes Ernest is Lecturer in English and Didactics at the Faculty of Education of Ramon Llull University in Barcelona, Spain. She has a degree in Linguistics from the University of Barcelona, Spain, and is currently working on her doctoral thesis, which focuses on the ways that heritage languages can be used in primary school language classrooms in order to promote plurilingual and intercultural competences among pupils. She has worked as a Lecturer in English, Translation and Interpreting at the University of Vic, Barcelona, and has also worked as an English and French language teacher in primary and secondary schools in Spain, France, South America, Pakistan and India. She is a member of the Research Group on Language and Intercultural Competence in Teaching and Learning Languages (CILCEAL), which focuses on the use of the L1/L1s and translation in language learning, CLIL, language acquisition in multilingual contexts and the use of children's literature as a learning strategy for developing intercultural competence. Her research interests include English language teaching, the use of the L1/L1s in the language classroom, plurilingualism and language visibility.
caterinase@blanquerna.url.edu

Foreword
Jim Cummins

Children's Literature in Multilingual Classrooms evoked powerful and conflicting emotions as I read its accounts of inspirational pedagogy implemented in diverse contexts with students and parents from many parts of the world. On the one hand, I was encouraged by the fact that educators were able to incorporate the rich multilingual resources represented by their school communities into classroom instruction and I was moved by the dramatic impact that these pedagogical initiatives had on students' and parents' sense of self and on their engagement with literacy. The image of students and their communities constructed in these pedagogical interactions challenges the stereotypical image of immigrant and minority group students and communities frequently held by members of the wider society and sometimes by educators themselves. Judith Oller (this volume), for example, documents the fact that for many Spanish educators the presence of immigrant students in their classrooms has been seen as a major problem. They locate the source of students' educational difficulties in presumed characteristics of the students themselves (e.g. poor study habits) or in attributes of their families (e.g. lack of interest in their children's education). The powerful intellectual work carried out by students of immigrant background, which many of the chapters in this book document so vividly, refute these stereotypical perceptions and demonstrate that students will develop what Patrick Manyak (2004) has termed *identities of competence* when instruction connects with their lives and affirms the legitimacy of their bilingual and bicultural identities.

On the other hand, however, I was troubled by the knowledge that policymakers would tend to dismiss the research described in these pages as largely irrelevant to policy because of its qualitative nature and lack of generalizability to instructional contexts beyond those described in the specific case studies or narrative accounts. It thus seemed relevant to sketch in this Foreword the claims to scientific credibility offered in the chapters of this volume.

It is worth noting initially that many of the educational policies enacted during the past 15 years in both the United Kingdom and the United States (to take just two examples) are largely devoid of empirical foundation or scientific credibility. There is no evidence, for example, that either 'synthetic phonics' (in the UK) or 'systematic phonics' (in the US) improves reading comprehension over the long term, and yet these constructs continue to dominate literacy policies in these contexts (see Cummins, 2007). In the US context, historian Diane Ravitch's (2013) book *Reign of Error* has comprehensively refuted the major claims underlying educational policies during both the Bush and Obama administrations. Policies in relation to literacy instruction, closing the achievement gap between social groups and combating the effects of poverty on attainment have all been based on ideological narratives that are blatantly inconsistent with empirical data and scientific analysis.

Clearly an ideological narrative also permeates the chapters in *Children's Literature in Multilingual Classrooms*. The authors endorse notions of equity in education, teaching the whole child, the school's role in valuing and expanding children's linguistic, intellectual and cultural capital and so on. The scientific issue is not whether this ideological orientation is appropriate but rather to what extent its associated theoretical propositions are *adequate* to explain the research data. A related criterion for judging any set of theoretical propositions, such as those advanced explicitly or implicitly in the present volume, is how *useful* they are to guide instructional practice in ways that will improve achievement. Thus, *adequacy* refers to the extent to which theoretical claims are consistent with the empirical data and provide a coherent and comprehensive account of the data, while *usefulness* refers to the extent to which these theoretical ideas can be used effectively by educators to implement the educational policies and practices they imply or prescribe.

In contrast to the theoretical claims underlying many mainstream literacy policies, even a cursory examination of the empirical data demonstrates that the claims advanced in this volume are both adequate to account for the data and also directly useful to educators who are committed to implement effective practice. In the sections below, I consider three of the theoretical claims that underlie the instructional initiatives discussed in this volume and examine the extent to which they are consistent with the broader empirical data. These theoretical claims entail major implications for advancing the academic achievement of bilingual and socially marginalized students and thus merit serious consideration from policymakers and educators.

Claim 1. Acknowledging and promoting bilingual students' home languages (L1) within the mainstream classroom supports students in transferring knowledge across languages and enhances their awareness of language and expertise in using language. Obviously the use of dual language books and the incorporation of students' home languages into the instructional process contravenes the conventional wisdom that we should maximize students' exposure to the dominant school language and also keep bilinguals' two (or more) languages separate to avoid confusion between them (e.g. in the process of acquiring decoding skills). Fortunately, there is not a shred of evidence for either of these assumptions. We know that there is extensive transfer across languages with respect to concepts, learning strategies, metalinguistic awareness, phonological awareness, morphological awareness and, for languages with shared histories, specific linguistic elements (e.g. cognates). Even languages as different as Chinese and English show strong cross-lingual relationships. For example, a large-scale study involving 30,000 Grade 9 students in Taiwan by Hui-Kai Chuang and colleagues (2012) found that 60 per cent of the variance in English reading scores could be explained by Mandarin reading scores.

The process of cross-lingual transfer and the importance of developing literacy in L1 can be seen in action in the following account of a Grade 2 student which was shared with me by Frances Bekhechi, a teacher at the International School of Brussels:

> We're in the throes of portfolio conferences at the moment and I was working with one of our little 2nd graders, helping her prepare what she was going to share with her parents. (This child was a complete beginner in September). The reading section of her portfolio had a very simple text that she was able to read earlier in the year, as well as a much more advanced one that she can read now. (She has made amazing progress). It also included a reflection sheet which she had to fill in, describing what she saw as her successes, challenges and next steps. She identified her challenges as being 'reading harder words'. When I asked her what she thought she could do to help her with this challenge, she said: 'Get books with English on one page and Chinese on the other page. When there's a hard word in English, you look at the Chinese and it help you understand.' (We're still working on the '-s' on the third person!)
>
> (Frances Bekhechi, personal communication, 18 March 2011)

In addition to the extensive evidence of cross-lingual transfer, the research also demonstrates that development of bilingual skills results in a variety of cognitive advantages for bilinguals such as greater ability to focus on tasks, greater metalinguistic awareness and more success in acquiring additional languages (see Adesope *et al.* (2010) for a review of this research).

Thus, although the research described in this volume does not directly establish cognitive advantages for bilingual students nor show evidence of cross-linguistic transfer beyond the specific contexts investigated, it does illustrate vividly through the insights and writing of children and parents how these processes operate. The research also highlights innovative instructional strategies that promote two-way cross-linguistic transfer and enhancement of students' awareness of language and how it operates.

Claim 2. Literacy engagement promotes literacy attainment. The case studies documented in this volume demonstrate how literacy engagement among bilingual students is enhanced when: (a) dual language books are available and used in the classroom; (b) parents become involved in reading dual language or L1 books either in the classroom or at home with their own children; (c) students engage in writing their own dual language books using all of their linguistic or plurilingual resources to translate from L1 to L2 or vice versa. The case studies also show that when the use of L1 is legitimized in the classroom, newcomer students are enabled to engage in creative writing. Teachers can usually find a way (through people or technology) to help students translate their L1 writing into the major school language.

Why is it important to enhance students' literacy engagement? Literacy engagement has emerged in multiple studies (both quantitative and qualitative) as perhaps the most significant determinant of literacy attainment. This is not the place to review this research in any detail. Interested readers can find documentation for this claim for both L1 and L2 in many research reports from around the globe (e.g. Elley, 1991; Neuman, 1999; OECD, 2010; Sullivan and Brown, 2013). The OECD data, involving hundreds of thousands of 15-year-old students in many countries, has shown that approximately one-third of the association between reading performance and student socio-economic background was mediated by reading engagement. The implication is that schools can significantly reduce the negative effects of socio-economic disadvantage by ensuring that students have access to a rich print environment and become actively engaged with literacy. In the case of newcomer students, teachers can help students engage with literacy during the period when they are still acquiring basic literacy skills in the school language by encouraging them to read and write in their L1 and/or create dual language texts.

The research demonstrating the centrality of literacy engagement for the development of reading and writing abilities reinforces the legitimacy of the pedagogical initiatives described in this volume. These initiatives, however, go beyond the quantitative research by demonstrating the strong relationships that exist between identity investment and literacy engagement. The literature and art created by students (and parents) holds a mirror up to them in which their identities are reflected back in a positive light. When students create identity texts in their two (or more) languages, they are showcasing their evolving bilingualism and biliteracy as an intellectual accomplishment valued within their school communities.

Teachers can promote the development of identities of competence associated with literacy by engaging students in discussion about the purposes and the power of literacy. This was brought home to me during a visit to a highly diverse primary school in the Toronto District School Board some years back. In one of the classes, students had responded to the sentence starter *Reading makes me powerful because ...* and had posted their responses outside the classroom. Here are Tasneem's thoughts about the power of reading:

> Reading makes me powerful because ...
>
> When I grow up I can find a better job than people who can't read. Somebody can also trick you to do something that will get you in trouble.
>
> Reading gives you new words to learn. It gives my brain new ideas. It helps your vocabulary so when you need to write something you can use longer and harder words. In school you can get a better mark using more words.

Clearly, Tasneem does not lack motivation to read. For her, engagement with literacy is identity-affirming, as it is for the multilingual students whose experiences are documented in this volume.

Claim 3. Identity affirmation is a prerequisite for academic engagement. Extensive research has been carried out by sociologists and anthropologists on issues related to ethnicity and educational achievement (see Cummins and Early (2011) for a review). These studies point clearly to the centrality of societal power relations in explaining historical and current achievement patterns among students from socially marginalized groups. Ladson-Billings expresses the point succinctly with respect to African-American students: 'The problem that African-American students face is the constant devaluation of their culture both in school and in the larger society' (1995: 485). A direct implication is that in order to reverse this pattern of underachievement, educators, both individually and collectively, must challenge the operation of coercive power relations in the classroom interactions they orchestrate with marginalized group students.

The pedagogical initiatives described in this volume illustrate how educators *can* challenge coercive relations of power. The interactions they orchestrate with students affirm students' identities, thereby promoting *empowerment*, understood as the *collaborative creation of power*. Power is generated in teacher–student interactions such that students (and teachers) feel more affirmed in their linguistic, cultural and intellectual identities and more confident in their ability to succeed in school. For example, the incorporation of students' L1 into classroom instruction challenges the devaluation of their language and culture in the wider society. Instruction that validates students' L1 as a cognitive tool connects to their lives and the funds of knowledge in their communities, affirms their bilingual and bicultural identities, and enables them to express their intelligence at an age-appropriate level.

The centrality of negotiating identities in ways that generate empowerment is lucidly expressed by Canadian First Nations high school student Cassandra Bice-Zaugg in reflecting on the visual art and poetry that she and her classmates created as they worked with Ojibwe artist and elder, Rene Meshake:

> Take away identity and what do you have? If you have a student that doesn't know who they are, do you think they care about what goes on in the classroom?
>
> (Cassandra Bice-Zaugg, Mississauga of the New Credit First Nations, Ontario, in Montero *et al.*, 2013: 90)

In conclusion, the pedagogical initiatives documented in this volume establish phenomena that require scientific explanation. They refute a variety of 'common sense' assumptions and theoretical claims that continue to influence educational policies in many countries. Among these claims are the arguments that immigrant and minority group students' L1 is a cause of underachievement and that students' literacy skills will be most successfully promoted by maximizing exposure to the dominant language at school (e.g. Esser, 2006). In opposition to these claims, the chapters in this volume demonstrate that students *can* engage actively with literacy even when their knowledge of the dominant school language is limited; they also provide multiple examples both of two-way transfer across languages as students grapple with academic tasks and increasing metalinguistic awareness arising from bringing the two languages into productive contact (e.g. through translation of stories from one language to another). Above all, they demonstrate that students will engage actively with literacy only to the extent that such engagement is identity-affirming. Creative writing and other forms of cultural production (e.g. art, drama, music, etc.) represent an *expression* of identity, a *projection* of identity into new social spheres and a *re-creation* of identity as a result of feedback from and dialogue with multiple audiences. This transformation of student identities becomes possible when educators exercise their agency and choose to teach the whole child.

Jim Cummins
Toronto, March 2014

References

Adesope, O.O., Lavin, T., Thompson, T. and Ungerleider, C. (2010) 'A systematic review and meta-analysis of the cognitive correlates of bilingualism'. *Review of Educational Research*, 80 (2), 207–45.

Chuang, H.-K., Joshi, R. and Dixon, L. (2012) 'Ninth-grade adolescents' cross-language transfer of reading ability: Evidence from Taiwanese'. *Journal of Literacy Research*, 44 (1), 97–119.

Cummins, J. (2007) 'Pedagogies for the poor? Re-aligning reading instruction for low-income students with scientifically based reading research'. *Educational Researcher*, 36 (9), 564–72.

Cummins, J. and Early, M. (2011) *Identity Texts: The collaborative creation of power in multilingual schools*. Stoke-on-Trent: Trentham Books.

Elley, W.B. (1991) 'Acquiring literacy in a second language: The effect of book-based programs'. *Language Learning*, 41 (3), 375–411.

Esser, H. (2006) *Migration, language and integration* (AKI Research Review 4). Berlin: Programme on Intercultural Conflicts and Societal Integration (AKI), Social Science Research Center. Online. www2000.wzb.eu/alt/aki/files/aki_research_review_4.pdf (accessed 29 May 2014).

Ladson-Billings, G.J. (1995) 'Toward a theory of culturally relevant pedagogy'. *American Education Research Journal*, 32 (3), 465–91.

Manyak, P.C. (2004) '"What did she say?" Translation in a primary-grade English immersion class'. *Multicultural Perspectives*, 6 (1), 12–18.

Montero, M.K., Bice-Zaugg, C., Marsh, A.C.J. and Cummins, J. (2013) 'Activist literacies: Validating Aboriginality through visual and literary identity texts'. *Journal of Language and Literacy Education*, 9 (1), 73–94. Online. http://jolle.coe.uga.edu/wp-content/uploads/2013/06/Validating-Aboriginality.pdf (accessed 29 May 2014).

Neuman, S.B. (1999) 'Books make a difference: A study of access to literacy'. *Reading Research Quarterly*, 34 (3), 286–311.

OECD (2010) *PISA 2009 Results: Learning to learn: Student engagement, strategies and practices (Volume III)*. Paris: OECD. Online. www.oecd.org/dataoecd/11/17/48852630.pdf (accessed 29 May 2014).

Ravitch, D. (2013) *Reign of Error: The hoax of the privatization movement and the danger to America's public schools*. New York: Alfred A. Knopf.

Sullivan, A. and Brown, M. (2013) *Social Inequalities in Cognitive Scores at Age 16: The role of reading*. London: Centre for Longitudinal Studies, Institute of Education, University of London. Online. www.cls.ioe.ac.uk (accessed 29 May 2014).

Introduction
Christine Hélot

The concept of this book originated from a colloquium organized at the International Symposium on Bilingualism (ISB) in Oslo in June 2011, entitled *Children's Literature, Translation and Bilingual Pedagogy: A critical approach to the teaching of literacy in multilingual contexts*. The colloquium brought together researchers in the field of children's literature, bilingual pedagogy, multiliteracy and translation studies who had discussed and debated their research together in many previous conferences and symposia (Association Internationale de Linguistique Appliquée, British Association of Applied Linguistics, British Educational Research Association, Multilingual Europe). It was the first time, however, that the topic of children's literature related to multilingualism and multiliteracy was included in an ISB conference.

This book brings together the stories of learning communities from different parts of the globe (Austria, Catalonia, Canada, Finland, New Zealand, the United Kingdom) who are engaged in developing new pedagogical approaches to literacy teaching in multilingual classrooms through the use of children's literature. Despite a substantial amount of research on literacy since the pioneering publications of the New London Group (1996) on biliteracy (Hornberger, 2003; Kenner, 2004; Sneddon, 2009; Cummins and Early, 2011) and on bi- and multilingual pedagogy (Garcia, 2008; Cummins, 2000; Cummins, 2007; Cummins and Early, 2011), it is still difficult for teachers to move beyond the traditional monoglossic approach (Garcia, 2009) used for teaching children to read and write in the national language. It is even more difficult, in view of the heterogeneity of languages and cultures present in twenty-first-century classrooms, to convince teachers to include in their literacy activities languages and cultures they do not know (Hélot, 2011).

However, many teachers all over the world do develop innovative literacy projects even when constrained by top-down curricula and a growing educational culture of testing. The development of new technologies has also changed our educational landscapes and our literacy practices outside of classrooms. But despite computers, the world wide web, interactive whiteboards and social media, the 'art' of teaching children to read and write remains mostly confined to the classroom context and enmeshed in pedagogical debates that do not necessarily take into account a wider picture.

We now have a better understanding of the role of the written word in our present-day society. We know that learning to read is learning to read the world. In other words, learning to read and write is about finding one's place in society, about understanding who we are, about opening possibilities to create new relationships, new identities, and about developing an awareness of the power language gives us to act in our world. But we are also faced with new challenges which all play their part in our contemporary classrooms: mobility, migration, linguistic and cultural diversity, and a growing awareness of social inequalities. These factors call into question our teaching approaches and the grounding of traditional literacy approaches. This implies a shift of perspective on the part of teachers that is far more demanding than most educators imagine (Mary and Young, 2010; Sneddon, present volume). It means teachers have to change their relationship to language – in the singular and in the plural – and to welcome a variety of languages that all have different functions in the lives of their students, including home languages, the language(s) of schooling, foreign languages, minority languages and endangered languages; in other words, transforming their monolingual classrooms into spaces where a multiplicity of languages are used for learning to read and write.

This book is about literacy teaching and learning in multilingual classrooms, classrooms where more than one language is used to learn to read and write and where the plurilingual repertoires of students are envisaged as plurilingual competence and thus as a learning resource. It is also about learning communities coming together to develop multilingualism into a pedagogy of multiliteracy. This means that teachers no longer have to rely solely on their knowledge of various languages but can draw on their students' knowledge, the knowledge of students' parents and the wider community, as well as sources available on the web. It is this pooling together of resources (or *crowdsourcing* linguistic resources, as Lotherington terms it in her chapter) that makes it possible to cross the traditional borders of learning within the confines of one language only, while at the same time developing a more socially embedded experience of literacy acquisition in school contexts.

The nine chapters in this book address literacy/multiliteracy pedagogy from different theoretical perspectives, including translation studies, biliteracy education, multiliteracies and multimodal approaches, Freire (1970) and Freinet (ICEM, 2013) pedagogies and participatory literacy. Imagining new pedagogies of bi- and multiliteracy means developing multiple visions of the teaching of reading and writing. The prefix *multi* lies at the heart of these new approaches, which can only be multilingual and multimodal, taking into account the fluidity of linguistic practices today, the complexity of the cultural contexts in which literacy practices take place, the hybridity of identities, the multimodality of digitally mediated communication and the breadth of linguistic diversity present in our classrooms.

From translation to translanguaging in children's literature

The notions of culture and interculturality are at the heart of the first three chapters, which raise central issues in translation studies and children's literature. The topic of translation also runs through most of the other chapters because it cannot be disassociated from multilingualism. Lyster, for example, describes teachers working on the same children's story in French and English – therefore one version is a translation – in order to focus on cross-lingual connections between the two languages and to foster bilingual language growth. Sneddon studies children engaged in the process of learning to read with dual language books; how they are able to negotiate meaning between their two languages, and how they transfer skills from both languages. This is made possible through translation, and indeed the children under study became the translators of their own texts. In the Sámi project (Pitkänen-Huhta and Pietikäinen), the children wrote their Little Books first in the two Sámi languages of the classroom and then were asked to choose the target languages for the translations. In this case community members were called upon for translation but the children chose the languages they wished to see displayed in their books. In the projects described by Sugranyes Ernest and González Davies, and Oller, as well as those by Pitkänen-Huhta and Pietikäinen, translation gave visibility and materiality to endangered languages and cultures, it allowed for these languages to be included in learning activities and it brought greater linguistic and cultural awareness. It is through the process of translation that different languages and cultures are mediated and made available to readers all over the world. Translation therefore 'involves far more than just the transfer from one language to another, it is a form of literary acknowledgement which allows for the circulation of literary works across the world and the development of a global literary heritage' (Hélot, 2011: 50).

González Davies's chapter offers great insight into the political and ideological role that the translation of children's stories has played in the revival of the Catalan language and identity throughout the twentieth century. We are given to understand how translators can be 'active agents of social, literary and linguistic transformation' in a given community. We also discover that the medium of children's literature can be used to implement language shift, as was the case in Catalonia. In Catalonia again, Sugranyes Ernest and González Davies argue for a reassessment of translation in language education to support language learning at school (convincingly shown in Lyster's chapter) and to develop intercultural competence. Through knowledge of two (or more) languages and cultures, learning to translate means learning to mediate different visions of the world and different ideologies of language.

This point is illustrated further in Daly's chapter. She interviewed New Zealand authors and translators of picture books published in English and in the Māori language who chose to use Māori loanwords in their translations and in texts written originally in English, or decided not to. As well as interpreting the growing trend to use loanwords as a sign of the increase in the vitality of the Māori language, as in González Davies's chapter, Daly examines the role of children's literature in legitimating minority languages and cultures. Interestingly, the choice of not translating but of borrowing words from Māori into English gives us examples of translators crossing the boundaries of a national language and offering readers written instances of translanguaging (Garcia, 2009; Hélot, 2014). It is notable in this case that a dominant language like English is made to borrow from the minority language, giving the Māori language and culture a visibility which the reader cannot fail to notice.

New pedagogies of multiliteracy: Metalinguistic awareness, multimodality and funds of knowledge

What is a 'pedagogy of multiliteracy'? First, a pedagogy of multiliteracy is about understanding how learning through two or more languages differs from learning through one language only. Several chapters give us some insights into children encountering texts and stories in different languages and how they benefited cognitively from reflecting on similarities and differences between the two languages of instruction. In the case of Sneddon's chapter, the young learners acquired reading competence through being exposed to both of their languages; in Lyster's research they improved their vocabulary knowledge in the two languages of instruction, French and English. It should be made clear that in both studies specific biliteracy tasks were developed by teachers/researchers such as, for example, inviting learners to consciously make cross-lingual connections between their two languages. For the transfer of competence from one language to the other to be effective, learners must be supported in their investigation of the functioning of language. As argued by Cummins (2000) and Lyster (in this book), they must be taught about two-way cross-lingual transfer (L1 to L2 and L2 to L1) and they must be asked to focus not only on content but also on form, in the latter case on the structure of words in the two languages. Therefore a pedagogy of bi- or multiliteracy implies designing strategies of language instruction that do not leave the learners to make connections between their languages themselves, but that sustain them in their understanding of the way in which they draw on their plurilingual competence to learn to read and write.

A pedagogy of multiliteracy goes beyond the monoglossic ideology of language that is still prevalent not only in most foreign language classrooms but also in bilingual programmes where the two languages are kept strictly apart, each in their own space and time and distributed across school subjects. Bilingual programmes can also be constraining in classrooms where students speak languages other than the two languages of instruction. Clearly one can understand teachers struggling to find time and space to stretch their bilingual pedagogy and include more languages. However, there is something of a paradox in asking multilingual learners to silence some of their languages in a bilingual classroom.

Lotherington's chapter gives us an example of a pedagogical solution to this issue: in a bilingual programme in Canada, teachers devised literacy activities that included the two languages of instruction as well as the students' home languages. They developed a multiliteracy pedagogy that supported both the acquisition of literacy and their learners' plurilingual repertoire. Based on traditional children's stories, the literacy task involved rewriting these narratives in numerous languages using digital media with various communicative modalities, pictures, voice-over, sound and animation. Adding a further dimension to the multiliteracy pedagogy, Lotherington explains the potential for implementing a multimodal approach to literacy learning. Multimodality has come to have a wider meaning since the rapid development of ICT: young children (and their teachers) are confronted with new experiences of reading every day on the internet, deciphering the combined meanings of texts, pictures, photographs, video, music and various semiotic representations. However, although these experiences of new media give children different and complex experiences of reading, they are not always acknowledged or considered legitimate in the traditional classroom. Yet, as Lotherington explains, these new media are the very means through which the children develop their reading and writing competence while using their multiple languages.

Multimodality often goes along with multilingualism on the web, where different languages coexist peacefully and where minority languages have also been given some visibility, even if the hegemony of English cannot be ignored. The web also offers multilingual children new opportunities to visit sites in their home languages or to communicate regularly with their family, for example, through Skype or FaceTime. Families are the focus of Oller's chapter, in which we see immigrant mothers from Africa being invited by a library in Catalonia to produce bilingual storybooks in their home languages as well as in Catalan. Based on the notion of funds of knowledge, the objective of the project was to involve parents of different cultures in creating pedagogical resources for libraries, homes and schools. In the context of heritage languages, home literacy practices, like digital literacies, are rarely considered legitimate in school contexts. As Oller argues, this can have negative effects on the school performance of students of immigrant background. Therefore a pedagogy of multiliteracy is a pedagogy that empowers families to have an impact on the educational success of their children; it has a participatory dimension where actors from different spheres come together to implement community projects that impact on children's learning at school; it is inclusive of difference because different cultures are negotiated creatively and discontinuities between home and school are bridged. It is ecological in the sense that languages associated with migration, and often seen as having low status, become valued as literacy resources in institutional spaces such as schools and libraries.

Multiliteracy pedagogy in practice: Children as authors

This book is about learning to read and write in several languages and in different semiotic modes, but it is also about literature. All the authors writing here consider children's literature as a central means to familiarize children with the written word, with narratives, with creativity and with meaning making. But instead of working with children's books written in only one language, as is the norm in most classrooms, they move beyond the boundaries of one language/one culture. They describe pedagogical strategies that engage children in reading and writing in several languages and in understanding what it means to move from one language to another, in other words, to translate. They give examples of activities where learners are taught to negotiate meaning for those who do not know the language in question and to build bridges between different cultures.

In the third part of this book, and this is by no means the least important point, the reader will discover another dimension of multiliteracy pedagogy, one in which children are encouraged to become the *authors* of their own books, as well as in some cases the *makers* of their own books. The reader will also understand how, through this process, children became the creators of their own learning materials. In Sneddon's longitudinal study of children in multilingual classrooms in east London, we follow bilingual learners becoming biliterate and working in groups to develop bilingual stories that will become literacy resources for the school. We also see teachers questioning the monoglossic policy of English as the main medium of education, and using dual language books written in English and in the learners' heritage languages. Here again, participatory literacy is developed, with home–school relationships being strengthened and heritage languages legitimized for multiliteracy development.

In Finland and Austria, children were also engaged in writing their own stories in a variety of formats (dual language, bi- and multilingual, translated, on paper and using new media) and in a multiplicity of languages: their own, other children's and even invented languages. As in Sneddon's project, young learners invested their identity in producing rich narratives, which they illustrated and produced in the format of Little Books. In both contexts they were engaged in literacy activities which were close to real-world tasks. The aim of the Little Books project is to create a collection to be distributed beyond schools, in libraries and in homes. In Finland the books produced by the children were professionally printed, and a book launch was organized to showcase their creativity. In Finland and Austria the Little Books have become famous: the Sámi books were presented in the Parliament, and in Vienna they attracted journalists and famous visitors.

The Little Books in Finland were developed to provide support for increasing the value of endangered Sámi languages, to help their revitalization and to develop resources for Sámi medium education. In their analysis of the Little Books project Pitkänen-Huhta and Pietikäien make a convincing case for the possibility of developing meaningful multiliteracy activities even when the learners have limited linguistic resources. Also enlightening are the discussions about the wide choice of target languages for translation and the community's involvement in the translation process, providing yet another example of participatory literacy.

In the Austrian context, over five hundred titles of the Little Books have been produced to date in a very wide range of languages. They were produced in a multilevel class of young newcomer students in Vienna. The Little Books format is simple and has been very successful. Most are created by children working collaboratively, inside or outside the classroom, and they are produced in a range of different genres, including non-fiction texts. Interestingly, while most of the books are bilingual, the children are not expected to write in more than one language: they are free to choose from their plurilingual repertoire any language they prefer. The teachers were wary of the danger of making multilingualism exotic and preferred to acknowledge linguistic diversity as part of everyday life in the twenty-first century.

The Little Books in Finland and Austria are examples of what a pedagogy of multiliteracy means: through the empowerment of minority speakers' literacy competence, and the development of new understandings of literacy acquisition, less culturally hegemonic literacy practices can develop in schools and more inclusive approaches to dominated languages and cultures are fostered. The Little Books are examples of children's literature produced by the children themselves, of children's voices being heard and of learning resources being shared with peers, teachers, families and the wider community.

Children's literature today provides us with an incredible wealth of talented authors and illustrators who no longer underestimate their young audience as readers, and who call upon their creativity to engage them in meaning making of a highly complex nature. Indeed, many of these authors encourage young readers to become authors and illustrators themselves. Some of those who are themselves multilingual have even dared to venture into translanguaging (Hélot, 2014). Lately, publishers have decided to provide more dual language books, multilingual collections of poetry and stories that encourage children to learn to read and write in different alphabets, giving teachers more resources for their multilingual classrooms. And there are also new media programs being developed to help students produce multilingual texts in classrooms (for example, see www.scribjab. com, developed at Simon Fraser University in Vancouver).

Perhaps central to all these new developments is the focus on creativity: creativity in using language and languages beyond the traditional borders of the monolingual classroom; creativity in building less essentialized visions of language(s) when teaching literacy; creativity in understanding the complex relationship between language and identity and creativity in imagining new pedagogical approaches to reading and writing that will nurture learners throughout their lives, and open the doors to their own talents.

We hope readers of this volume will be inspired by the wide spectrum of pedagogical possibilities designed to empower multilingual learners in the development of their literacy acquisition in multiple languages. We hope it will give them the incentive to imagine innovative approaches to literacy teaching in our multilingual, multimodal world of reading and writing. And we hope that researchers and teacher educators will take these critical approaches to literacy teaching further, to explore new understandings of the role of reading and writing in the lives of our children and grandchildren.

References

Cummins, J. (2000) *Language Power and Pedagogy: Bilingual children in the crossfire*. Clevedon: Multilingual Matters.

— (2007) 'Rethinking monolingual instructional strategies in the multilingual classroom'. *The Canadian Journal of Applied Linguistics*, 10 (2), 221–40.

Cummins, J. and Early, M. (eds) (2011) *Identity Texts: The collaborative creation of power in the multilingual classroom*. Stoke-on-Trent: Trentham Books.

Freire, P. (1970) *Pedagogy of the Oppressed*. New York: Continuum.

Garcia, O. (2008) 'Multilingual language awareness and teacher education'. In Hornberger, N. (ed.) *Encyclopedia of Language and Education, Vol. 6: Knowledge about language*. New York: Springer, 385–400.

— (2009) *Bilingual Education in the 21st Century: A global perspective*. Malden, MA: Wiley Blackwell.

Gregory, E. (2008) *Learning to Read in a New Language*. London: Sage.

Hélot, C. (2011) 'Children's literature in the multilingual classroom: Developing multiliteracy acquisition'. In Hélot, C. and O'Laoire, M. (eds) *Language Policy for the Multilingual Classroom: Pedagogy of the possible*. Bristol: Multilingual Matters, 42–64.

— (2014) 'Rethinking bilingual pedagogy in Alsace: Translingual writers and translanguaging'. In Blackledge, A. and Creese, A. (eds) *Heteroglossia as Practice and Pedagogy* (Educational Linguistics Vol. 20). Dordrecht: Springer, 217–38.

Hornberger, N.H. (ed.) (2003) *Continua of Biliteracy: An ecological framework for educational policy, research and practice in multilingual settings*. Clevedon: Multilingual Matters.

ICEM/Institut Coopératif de l'École Moderne. Pédagogie Freinet (2013) *Éléments de théorisation de la pédagogie Freinet: Une approche complexe des apprentissages*. Vol. 1. Nantes: Laboratoire de Recherche Coopérative, Éditions ICEM Pédagogie Freinet.

Kenner, C. (2004) *Becoming Biliterate: Young children learning to write different writing systems*. Stoke-on-Trent: Trentham Books.

Mary, L. and Young, A. (2010) 'Preparing teachers for the multilingual classroom: Nurturing reflective, critical awareness'. In Ehrhart, S., Hélot, C. and Le Nevez, A. (eds) *Plurilinguisme et formation des enseignants: Une approche critique/ Plurilingualism and Teacher Education: A critical approach*. Frankfurt: Peter Lang, 195–219.

New London Group (1996) 'A pedagogy of multiliteracies: Designing social factors'. *Harvard Educational Review*, 66 (1), 60–92.

Sneddon, R. (2009) *Bilingual Books – Biliterate Children: Learning to read through dual language books*. Stoke-on-Trent: Trentham Books.

Part One

From translation to
translanguaging in
children's literature

1

Chapter 1

The changing role of translators in a bilingual context

Catalan (in)visibility and the translation of children's literature

Maria González Davies

Introduction

Translated books are often read and used in the classroom without further thought about the underlying ideology or decisions taken by the translator. These decisions are often unconscious, driven by what Gideon Toury (1995) calls the 'norms' of translation, which may be influenced by social, historical, economic or ideological factors. Alternatively, they may be conscious when the translator – or the publisher – decides to adopt a specific approach to the translation process. Translation is not as innocent a practice as it may seem. However, 'the illusion of non-interference', in Pokorn's words (2012), persists.

One of the main dilemmas usually faced by the translator is whether to transfer the source text so that it is near to the target audience (i.e. to domesticate the text) or, on the contrary, to keep as close to the source text as possible even though this may involve a certain feeling of 'strangeness' for the target reader, especially regarding cultural references and wordplay (i.e. to 'foreignize' the text). Reasons for and against each of these two options have been put forward and the most relevant for our purposes will be dealt with later in the chapter. Furthermore, the translator's job is to spot and solve translation problems, including cultural references, humour and poetry, by applying suitable translation strategies using both creative and critical thinking skills in an informed way. Finally, translation may serve different functions, from endorsing censorship practices to becoming a key tool for the revival of minority languages and literatures, as was the case in several countries such as Finland and Catalonia at the turn of the twentieth century (Bacardí *et al.*, 1998; Carner, 1970; González Davies, 2002; Oittinen, 2000; Oittinen, 2003; Oliva, 1995; Parcerisas, 1997).

Translation choices, therefore, are loaded. They depend on many variables and norms, such as the social, cultural and economic background of a community, or its values, beliefs and images of childhood, all of which may influence the translator's individual choices. Consequently, translators may become active social agents, far from the passive role that they are usually assigned. This makes translation a complex activity that requires professional skills and extensive consideration, especially when dealing with children's and young adults' literature, which has often been used as a didactic and even political instrument to help shape new generations in certain contexts (González Davies, 2002; González Davies, 2011; González Davies, 2012; Hélot and O'Laoirie, 2011; Oittinen, 2000; Shavit, 2009; Van Collie and Verschueren, 2006). I argue that, as teachers, we should bear in mind the pedagogical – and even ideological – implications of choosing a translated text for our students without having considered these issues, as we may be presenting a loaded or biased image of the Other. This issue will be explored as the chapter unfolds.

In light of the above, this chapter presents an historical overview of the role of translators and translation in a so-called minority culture, specifically regarding the reception of children's and young adults' literature in Catalan. The underlying argument is that, at the turn of the twentieth century, translation was consciously adopted as a means to favour a revival of the language and literature, to regain and re-establish an identity alongside the majority language, Spanish, and that translation continues to occupy a central place in Catalan culture. This will be illustrated through the analysis of two translations into Catalan of Lewis Carroll's *Alice in Wonderland*, one undertaken near the beginning (1927) and one near the end (1996) of the twentieth century.

General sociolinguistic background: (How) has Catalan survived a major language, Spanish?

From the turn of the twentieth century up to the Spanish Civil War (1936–1939), Catalonia, a region in the north-east of Spain, was a mainly conservative community with a successful industry that made it stand out as a significant economic force. Its language became a crucial symbol of identity and successful efforts were made for its revival, including on the political front, with the *Lliga Regionalista*[1] claiming Catalan as a co-official language (Grau, 2006). This claim was not conceded by the central (Spanish) government, although Catalan was required to obtain a job in the local civil service. Paradoxically, from 1916 Catalan was forbidden to be used as the language of schooling. These approaches and actions symbolically converged in 1918 when Pompeu Fabra wrote the first Catalan grammar to lay down common norms (i.e. to 'normalize' the language). Moreover, the publishing houses turned out books both in Spanish and Catalan – another prosperous industry.

However, the Spanish Civil War put an end to this emerging *entente cordiale*. Catalan was forbidden under the Franco regime and its language and literature, which had started to do well once more, seemed to be doomed. Spanish became the only official language in all Spain, and other languages such as Basque/Euskera, Catalan and Galician were outlawed.

Has this situation altered at the turn of the twenty-first century? Spanish is one of the most widely spoken languages in the world, with approximately 400 million users, while Catalan is spoken by over 10 million people (Sorolla, 2012: 17–18; Ethnologue, 2013). In Catalonia Spanish and Catalan are now co-official languages and, in such a case, choosing to translate into the minority language had and has clear political and ideological implications. The fight against linguistic and cultural attrition came mainly through three actions during the twentieth century: the conscious use of translation of children's and young adults' literature, the support of the mass media and school immersion programmes.

The conscious use of translation of children's and young adults' literature

The translation of children's and young adults' literature emerged forcefully at the turn of the twentieth century and still occupies a central place in literary publications, although now this may also be considered to be part of a process of globalization. However, the thriving efforts at the turn of the twentieth century to increase publications in Catalan were annihilated after the Civil War when languages other than Spanish were forbidden and censorship was enforced. The conscious decisions of publishers, writers and translators at the turn of the twentieth century enabled the widespread diffusion and use of a language and literature that had been relegated to oral expression for centuries. Between 1868 and 1939, translated children's and young adults' literature became the means to introduce the language into society in such a way that parents, teachers and children could read in Catalan the classics that formed the literary heritage of other countries. Over twenty publishers specializing in children's and young adults' literature in Catalonia are recorded and a public library network with a section on children's and young adults' literature was set up in 1918 (Colomer, 2002; Rovira and Ribé, 1972).

In the 1920s, Catalan authors published many more translations than original works. In Rovira and Ribé's catalogue of children's literature (1972), which covers all children's publications up to 1939 in Catalan, over one hundred translations figure from several languages, including Russian, Arabic and Japanese. In addition, 85 collections of children's literature can be found, including stories, plays and journals. English, German and French literature were especially favoured, to the point where the practice of indirect translation was common and literature in English was often translated from French texts. The translator became a very visible and active agent of social, literary and linguistic transformation in the Catalan community while also existing within a strong Spanish context.

Moreover, although the message and effect of the translations very often served an ideological rather than a purely literary purpose, the translation of texts into Catalan also served to advance the use of two linguistic models that survive at the turn of the twenty-first century: (a) formal *preciosisme,* and (b) standard registers used in the mass media and everyday communication (Barba, 1997; Oliva, 1997; Pericay and Toutain, 1996). After the Spanish Civil War (1936--39) publications in Catalan practically disappeared until the 1960s.

Mass media

The *Ley de prensa* (Media Law) issued in 1964 tentatively opened doors again. It allowed for censorship to be lifted and more translations into Catalan were permitted, leading to popular and widespread publication in the present. Significant dates were chosen to mark the revival of Catalan in the media. For instance, *Avui,*[2] the first newspaper entirely in Catalan, was first published on 23 April 1976 (Saint George's Day, the patron saint of Catalonia). At present, seven newspapers are published,[3] five entirely in Catalan and two – the most widely read – in parallel bilingual editions. Catalan television broadcasting opened with TV3 on 10 September 1983 (the day before the National Day of Catalonia). Now three Catalan channels coexist. Finally, the main children's magazine written wholly in Catalan, *Cavall Fort,* appears fortnightly and has a print run of 25,000.

School immersion

In 1983 the Catalan Government Decree (DOGC No. 322, 22/04/1983) ruled that all subjects should be taught in Catalan. Spanish is now taught for three hours a week. This may change with the new Spanish Government draft bill that aims at including more Spanish in Catalan schools (Ley Orgánica para la Mejora de la Calidad Educativa (LOMCE), 29 June 2013). The aim, according to the Ministry of Education, is to remove the differences between the autonomous communities.[4] One of the means to do this is to endorse the primary use of Spanish in two cases. In the first, although significant differences between Spanish and Catalan may be observed depending on the domain of use (either 'study' or 'playground and family' domains), on the geographical area and on other factors, the official language of study in all Catalonia is Catalan, for both state and private schools. However, the draft bill for the new Law of Education states that 'there will be a Government subsidy for private schools that welcome students who cannot find a school with instruction in Spanish' (Article 6), which does not reflect reality as Catalan is also the language of instruction in private schools. Also the draft bill allows for a second case where Spanish and a foreign language are considered as core subjects, but not so the co-official regional languages, which, although compulsory, will be considered to be a subject of specialty. The Catalan Government argues that, in practice, this will bring about the eradication of a thirty-year-old education system in which Catalan is the language of immersion, whereas the Ministry of Education claims that the draft bill does not modify the status of Catalan[5] (December 2012).

According to the Anuari Estadístic de Catalunya (Annual Directory of Statistics in Catalonia) (2010), the general sociolinguistic conclusion is that Catalan has definitely gained ground in the last three decades and is now a co-official language along with Spanish. However, besides the LOMCE draft bill, there are points still to be overcome before the language can become completely 'normalized':

1. The written factor:
   Catalan is relatively easy to understand for a Romance language speaker, but is quite opaque regarding its orthographic practices: the phoneme-grapheme correspondence is quite complex. Therefore, there is a significant difference between the proportion of people who can understand/speak it and the proportion who can write it – 91.1 per cent and 52.7 per cent respectively (Sorolla, 2012: 17).

2. The age factor:
   School immersion has been a key factor in reviving the language. It is the older population, from 35 years old, who cannot write it as well as those who have learnt it at school. However, 83 per cent of the population over 65 regard Catalan as their mother tongue compared with only 45 per cent among 14 to 19 year olds, mainly due to the relative mobility of these groups.

3. The geographical factor:
   Catalan is the usual language for communication in the inland area,
   but not on the coast, due to a higher rate of immigration and tourism.
   Moreover, studies on prosodic varieties conclude that there are significant
   intra-urban differences as there are, for instance, in Barcelona (Benet *et al.*, 2011).

Despite the obvious shifts regarding the social and economic situation in
Catalonia at the turn of the twenty-first century, the role of translation of
children's and young adults' literature is still pivotal today. In both 2008
and 2009 Catalonia, with a strong publishing industry, held the highest
percentage of translations (from and into any language) in all of Spain:
41.8 per cent and 45.2 per cent for each year respectively (followed by the
Balearic Islands: 29 per cent and 21 per cent). In addition, 9.6 per cent of
all books published in Spain were in Catalan. In Spain, 10.9 per cent of
publications belonged to children's and young adults' literature, whereas in
Catalonia the percentage was 41.3 (Anuari Estadístic de Catalunya, 2010).
In 2012, this trend continued: in Catalonia 44.3 per cent of published
titles were devoted to literature, of which 43.2 per cent were books for
children. More than half (57.2 per cent) of the publications for children
were published in Spanish and almost a quarter (24 per cent) in Catalan and
Valencian. Of these, 24.2 per cent were translations, English being the most
translated language (41.7 per cent) (Instituto Nacional de Estadística, 2012:
3). So, the percentages in Catalonia both for translation and for children's
and young adults' literature are still higher than anywhere else in Spain.

Illustrating the sociohistorical background: *Alice in Wonderland* revisited

Two Catalan translations of Carroll's *Alice in Wonderland* (1865) – the
first by Josep Carner (1927) and the second by Salvador Oliva (1996) –
will be used to illustrate the different original sociolinguistic contexts
and the changes that have taken place over the last hundred years. The
translations have been studied mainly from the angle of the domesticating
and foreignizing translation strategies adopted to reflect different agendas
in both their verbal and visual expressions (González Davies, 2002). A
domesticating strategy is applied when the translator makes the text familiar
to the target readers, either by using cultural references that are close to
them (sociocultural level) or by adapting it by making the language fluent
and the translator invisible (sociotextual level) (Hatim, 1996). On the other
hand, a foreignizing strategy makes the translator visible and the text seem

'strange' to the reader because it is close to the source language and culture (Venuti, 1995).

Catalan *Noucentisme* was a cultural movement that officially began in 1906 and ended in 1923. It favoured order, a return to the essence of Catalan and Mediterranean culture, Classicism and Europeanism. One of its main characteristics was its focus on advancing Catalan language and literature, usually through the exploration of an ornate style consistent with an interest in poetry. The Catalan Government and artists worked together towards a conscious national revival. On the literary front, translation was initiated in the receiving minority culture, so it can be considered a subversive choice in that it signified the rebellion of the minority language,[6] which aimed at universality through the exaltation of its own culture aided by translations. That the readers should not 'complain that the translations provoke an indefinable "strangeness"' (Jordana, 1938, in Bacardí *et al.*, 1998: 121)[7] was not only welcomed but consciously sought. In this context, the translator was deemed 'an educator of the masses' and translating became the 'sacred duty' (Montoliu, 1908, in Bacardí *et al.*, 1998: 37) of the great writers of the time.

This approach to translation is clearly suggested by the term used in Catalan for domestication, *anostrament* or 'making ours', which is in line with the positive view of translation to be found in most peripheral cultures. Here we will see how domestication was applied consciously in Josep Carner's translation of Carroll's *Alice in Wonderland* (1865): *Alícia en terra de meravelles* (1927). In contrast, Salvador Oliva, living at a time when the language has a more solid tradition to sustain it than a century ago, clearly stated that he did not feel this need (Oliva, 1997) and therefore consciously included neutralizing and foreignizing strategies at the sociocultural and linguistic level in his translation.

Nida's well-known classification of cultural references has been used in this study to analyse the rendering of the cultural references in the translations. He divided cultural referents into five groups (Nida, 1964: 55): (a) *material*, related to everyday objects; (b) *ecological*, related to differences in the places, weather, flora, fauna and so on; (c) *social*, related to social organization and its artistic manifestations in the arts or literature and history; (d) *religious,* which are the ritualized and ideological manifestation of the previous group; and (e) *linguistic*, the tool that is needed to express the previous group and which, according to Nida, belongs to the cultural level. On the other hand, the following definition of 'cultural reference' – which broadens Nida's classification – was applied to adjust the selection process:

> Any kind of expression (textual, verbal, non-verbal or audiovisual) denoting any material, ecological, social, religious, linguistic or emotional manifestation that can be attributed to a particular community (geographic, socio-economic, professional, linguistic, religious, bilingual, etc.) and would be admitted as a trait of that community by those who consider themselves to be members of it. Such an expression may, on occasions, create a comprehension or a translation problem.
>
> (González Davies and Scott-Tennent, 2005: 28)

Table 1.1 presents a few examples of domesticated and foreignized translations. In all cases, the first column indicates the cultural references in the source text, the second column includes Carner's translation, and the third is Oliva's translation (backtranslations into English have been provided). The numbers indicate the pages in each edition.

Table 1.1: Examples of domesticated and foreignized translations

a) Material references		
- Food and drink		
cake (33)	coca (14)	pastís (16)
Backtranslation		
cake	*Catalan bread cake*	*cake*
b) Ecological		
- Animals		
Cheshire cat (83)	gat castellà (63)	gat de Cheshire (63)
Backtranslation		
Cheshire cat	*Castilian cat*	*Cheshire cat*

c) *Social references*

- Literature

'You are old, Father William ...' (69) (parody of a poem by Southey)	... versos de Mossèn Cinto (50)	'Sou vell, Pare Guillem ...(47)
Shakespeare (48)	homes il.lustres (30)	Shakespeare (29)

Backtranslation

'You are old, Father William ...'	... Father Cinto's verses... (reference to the Catalan poet Mossén Jacint Verdaguer (1863–1918))	You are old, Father William ...'
Shakespeare	Illustrious men	Shakespeare

History

William the Conqueror (41)	Napoleó (23)	Guillem el Conqueridor (23)

Backtranslation

William the Conqueror	Napoleon	William the Conqueror

d) *Religious:* religious referents which do not appear in the source text have been added in Carner's translation

Oh, dear! (25)	Ave Maria! (5)	Òndia! (9)

Backtranslation

Oh, dear!	Virgin Mary!	Wow!

---

e) Linguistic references

- Pride in Catalan language

... she quite forgot how to speak good English (35)	... s'oblidà de parlar català fí (15)	... no es va adonar que li fallava la gramàtica (17)

Backtranslation

... she quite forgot how to speak good English	*... she forgot to speak good Catalan*	*... she didn't realize that her grammar was incorrect*

- The masculine as generic gender in Carner contrasted with Oliva's updated politically correct use of the masculine and the feminine:

children (87)	infants (69)	nens i nenes (64)

Backtranslation

children	*infants*	*Boys and girls*

The systematic complete comparison confirmed the initial observations: of 70 cultural objects identified in the book, Carner domesticated 29 whereas Oliva did so with 10. The quantifiable result of this observation is shown in Table 1.2 (González Davies, 2002: 23).

Table 1.2: Domesticated and foreignized cultural references in Carner (1927) and Oliva (1996)

	Domestication	Foreignization	No correspondence between the source and target texts
T1 - Carner	29 (39.7%)	12 (16.6%)	7 (9.7%)
T2 - Oliva	10 (13.8%)	24 (32.8%)	4 (5.5%)

Revisiting illustrations: Anglada in Carner versus Tenniel in Oliva

A further question: what should the translator do with the non-linguistic elements of a text? Should they be 'translated'? This is a controversial topic for most translators. In Carner's translation, Lola Anglada (1892–1984) took John Tenniel's place, basing her drawings on *Noucentista* ideology and taking the reader to a Catalan and Mediterranean environment, thus further emphasizing the tendency to domesticate the text. Lola Anglada was the best-known Catalonian illustrator of children's books in the first part of the twentieth century. She also wrote books for children[8] and was a firm believer in *Noucentista* ideology because for her 'art was a means to feel and think one's country through images ... to walk towards an ideal, civilised and modern country' (Cirici, 1979, in Comas, 1992: 53). Oliva's translation, on the other hand, includes Tenniel's drawings, thus favouring the foreign illustrator. The two examples in Figure 1.1 will suffice to compare the effect of the pictures on Carner's and Oliva's readers.

Reproduced with kind permission of Editorial Joventut and Editorial Empúries

Figure 1.1: The tea party

Carroll's underlying nightmarish and nonsensical atmosphere comes across in Tenniel's Mad Hatter, a grotesque and clownish creature, who in Anglada's drawings has been transformed into a distinguished nineteenth-century gentleman. The other characters at the tea party have also been sweetened and we can see how an English cottage has become a Catalan *masia* (country house) surrounded by Mediterranean conifers and fruit trees; the tea party has become a *berenar* (afternoon snack) in a typical *pati de masia* (country house courtyard). Although Carner's text says *l'hora del te*, the teapot has become a coffee-pot, coffee being a much more common drink in Catalonia, so that an inconsistency has been established between text and illustration. In a second example (Figure 1.2), the choice of playing cards clearly illustrates the wish to domesticate.

Reproduced with kind permission of Editorial Joventut and Editorial Empúries

Figure 1.2: Playing cards

We can see that in both the verbal and the visual renderings, Carner's degree of domestication choices is clearly higher than Oliva's, who has either compromised or chosen a foreignized reference when addressing an audience with a wider background knowledge of British cultural references than that of Carner's target readers. This is further reinforced by the fact that the percentages in the study of sociocultural objects are in stark contrast: it seems that both translators have produced a text which is consistent with its social and linguistic period, thus conforming to Toury's notion of 'norms' (1995: 53–69) and confirming that non-interference in translation is indeed an illusion. Both translators chose a certain approach and certain strategies consciously, as their published articles and interviews – directly related to each of these translations – further testify. Therefore, it is not a question of judging 'good' or 'bad' translations, but of asking whether translators' choices are coherent with their aims.

Conclusion

This chapter set out to explore how translation depends on many factors besides the purely linguistic and how it may serve political, social and ideological norms. Here, the case of Catalonia and its will to revive its language and literature at the turn of the twentieth century has served to illustrate how translation, and especially that of children's and young adults' literature, can be considered to be a key means to achieve this aim. In this context, translation can be considered to be a linguistic and literary laboratory in which to experiment with language and create new ways of expression, helped by foreign texts that were adapted consciously and systematically, also allowing for the fact that indirect translations were quite common. Indeed, a century later, these efforts seem to have played a critical role in the 'normalized' situation of Catalan at present. Moreover, translation still plays a key role in Catalan literature alongside a wide range of autochthonous literary production. In order to illustrate these points, two translations of the same text carried out at the beginning and end of the twentieth century have been analysed, since each of these translations is a motivated choice which springs from a social, historical and linguistic background. Thus, it may also be inferred that, when choosing a translated book, it is not sufficient to be familiar with the author's background, but it is also necessary to know about that of the translator in order to reach an understanding of the process of translation and of the final rendering. Interestingly, and contrary to mainstream belief, domestication is not always an imposed or colonizing choice: in certain circumstances, it can serve as an efficient means to an end.

Specifically regarding Catalonia, an informed historical overview accompanied by a systematized analysis of translation products (Bacardí *et al.*, 1998; Barba, 1997; Carner, 1970; González Davies, 2002; Lluch, 2013; Mañà, 2010; Oliva, 1995; Oliva, 1997) seems to yield the following observations: at the turn of the twentieth century, translation and the translator were at the centre of the cultural system following, mainly, an ideological call that made their activity visible and prestigious. This high regard for the task of the translators continued through the century, although increased professionalization and the opening of 25 Faculties of Translation in Spain (four of which are in Catalonia), along with the more commercial function of translation at the turn of the twenty-first century, have put translation, and not so much the translator, at the centre of Catalan cultural activity.

The chosen strategic approach to translation in Catalonia at the beginning of the twentieth century was mainly to domesticate the source texts, supported by explanatory prefaces and footnotes to help make them familiar to the target readers, so as to introduce international literature in the community. Translation was used consciously as linguistic experimentation in a search for rules and a literary and cosmopolitan language known as *preciosisme*. However, although this kind of language prevails for certain literary texts and in formal registers, everyday exchanges and the press have adopted the language of later post-Civil War writers, who are certainly indebted to their *Noucentiste* precursors and often refer to them. In the present, in a different sociocultural environment, translation is mainly characterized by foreignizing practices, informed creative solutions that break the sought-after rules and apply intratextual problem-solving.

As to children's and young adults' literature in Catalonia, the low number of books written and translated at the beginning of the twentieth century has risen, giving way to a proliferation of original texts and translations, thus confirming the value of the work of the pioneers. Methods and approaches may have differed, but the positive feeling towards translation and children's and young adults' literature in Catalonia has not changed nor has its crucial role in upholding the language.

As an overall conclusion to bear in mind when choosing a book that has been translated into any language to use in our classes or for research purposes, we should take into account what kind of image of the source text and culture is mirrored within and, more to the point, the possible (motivated) choices behind the translator's rendering. If possible, before making a final decision regarding books to be used to discover other cultures, it is worth consulting the original text with the help of speakers of the source language. It is very inspiring to encourage children themselves to initiate the process; that is, if willing, children from or familiar with other cultures can suggest books to be read and provide information about the translations of the cultural references, for example. It is even more authentic to set up (intra- or interclass) collaborative translation projects where the children themselves become the translators of stories from other cultures with the help of their schoolmates and, hopefully, of their families. The strength of the activity will lie in the discussions around the words, expressions, illustrations and so on. It is not a question of producing perfect static translations, but of creating a dynamic intercultural atmosphere that transcends the classroom to embrace significant life experiences where different voices may meet on equal terms. This volume certainly provides exciting ideas and an informed framework for carrying this out.

Notes

[1] Between 1901 and 1923, this was the hegemonic political party in Catalonia. It represented moderate separatist Catalanism, the concerns of the industrial bourgeoisie, agrarian landowners and the middle classes. It drafted a project for self-government and backed the first Statute of Autonomy in Catalonia.

[2] *Avui* and *El Punt* merged into *El Punt Avui* in July 2011.

[3] According to the Oficina de Justificación de la Difusión the average print runs of the main newspapers entirely in Catalan for January to December 2012 are: *Ara* 30,485; *El Punt Avui* 34,636. Bilingual newspapers: *La Vanguardia* 202,488; there are no data for *El Periódico de Catalunya*, although the newspaper itself claims a print run of 168,911 in the Spanish edition (www.irbbarcelona.org/files/File/2012_02_21_ElPeriodico_IRBBarcelona_cast.pdf) and 53,795 for the Catalan

edition (March 2013) (www.iec.cat/activitats/documents/manuel_ribas.pdf). These data vary for the digital versions.

[4] Spanish Ministry of Education (www.mecd.gob.es/servicios-al-ciudadano-mecd/participacion-publica/cerrados/2013/lomce/20131210-boe.html).

[5] *LOMCE. Nota aclaratoria respecto a la lengua vehicular en la enseñanza en el Anteproyecto de Ley Orgánica para la Mejora de la Calidad Educativa* (Clarification regarding the language used in teaching in the Bill for the Improvement of Educational Quality) (www.mecd.gob.es/servicios-al-ciudadano-mecd/participacion-publica/lomce/20121207-lomce-nota.html).

[6] This would be especially true after the Spanish Civil War when translation once again became the means to fight official decrees against the use of the language (see Espasa, 2001; Parcerisas, 1997).

[7] All translations from Catalan are mine.

[8] In Rovira and Ribé (1972), Anglada appears as the author of 15 books and as the illustrator of another 18 up to 1939 only.

References

Anuari Estadístic de Catalunya 2009 (2010) *Institut d'Estadística de Catalunya. Generalitat de Catalunya.* Online. www.idescat.cat/cat/poblacio/poblcensling.html (accessed 23 July 2013).

Bacardí, M., Fontcuberta, J. and Parcerisas, F. (1998) *Cent anys de traducció al Català (1891–1991). Antologia.* Vic: EUMO.

Barba, C. (1997) 'Alícia al país de la modernitat'. *Avui*, 30 January, 1–3.

Benet, A., Lleó, C. and Cortés, S. (2011) 'Phrase boundary distribution in Catalan: Applying the prosodic hierarchy to spontaneous speech'. In Gabriel, G. and Lleó, C. (eds) *Intonational Phrasing in Romance and Germanic Cross-Linguistic and Bilingual Studies.* Amsterdam: John Benjamins 97–126.

Carner, J. (1970) 'De l'art de traduir'. In Manent, A. (ed.) *Teoria de l'ham poètic.* Barcelona: Edicions, 55–9.

— (1971) *Alícia en terra de meravelles*, originally 1927. Barcelona: Joventut.

Carroll, L. (1970) *Alice's Adventures in Wonderland*, originally 1865. In Gardner. M. (ed.) *The Annotated Alice.* Middlesex: Penguin.

Cirici, A. (1979) 'Lola Anglada i els mites'. *Cuadernos de Literatura Infantil y Juvenil*, 43, 51–4.

Colomer, T. (ed.) (2002) *La literatura infantil i juvenil catalana: Un segle de canvis.* Bellaterra: Institut de Ciències de l'Educació.

Comas, M. (1992) 'Lola Anglada, in memoriam'. *Cuadernos de Literatura Infantil y Juvenil*, 43, 5.

Espasa, E. (2001) *La traducció dalt de l'escenari* (Biblioteca de Traducció i Interpretació, 6). Vic: Eumo Editorial.

Ethnologue. World Languages (2013) Online. www.ethnologue.com (accessed 5 August 2013).

Fabra, P. (2010) *Obres completes de Pompeu Fabra: Gramàtiques 1918, 1946 i 1956*, originally 1918. Barcelona: Proa.

González Davies, M. (2002) 'Translating children's literature in a bilingual context: *Alice* in Catalan'. *The Knight Letter: The Lewis Carroll Society of North America*, 70, 12–16.

— (2011) 'Engaging future generations in multicultural projects through the translation of literature for young readers'. In Benert, B. and Clermont, P. (eds) *Contre l'innocence: Esthétique de l'engagement en littérature de jeunesse.* Frankfurt: Peter Lang, 439–51.

— (2012) 'The role of translation in other learning contexts: Towards acting interculturally'. In Borodo, M. and Hubscher-Davidson, S. (eds) *Global Trends in Translation and Interpreting*. London: Continuum, 161–79.

González Davies, M. and Scott-Tennent, C. (2005) 'A problem-solving and student-centred approach to the translation of cultural references'. *Meta: Journal des traducteurs/Meta: Translators' Journal*, 50 (1), 160–79.

Grau, J. (2006) *La Lliga Regionalista i la llengua Catalana, 1901–1924*. Barcelona: Publicacions de l'Abadia de Montserrat.

Hatim, B. (1996) 'Translation Studies'. Seminar presented at the Faculty of Translation and Interpreting, University of Vic, November.

Hélot, C. and O'Laoirie, M. (2011) *Language Policy for the Multilingual Classroom: Pedagogy of the possible*. Bristol: Multilingual Matters.

Instituto Nacional de Estadística (2012) *Publicaciones 2013*. Online. www.ine.es (accessed 5 August 2013).

Lluch, G. (2013) *La lectura en Catala per a infants i adolescents*. Barcelona: L'Abadia de Montserrat.

LOMCE (2013) *Nota aclaratoria respecto a la lengua vehicular en la enseñanza en el Anteproyecto de Ley Orgánica para la Mejora de la Calidad Educativa*. Online. www.mecd.gob.es/servicios-al-ciudadano-mecd/participacion-publica/ cerrados/2013/lomce/20121207-lomce-nota.html (accessed 6 June 2014).

Mañà, T. (2010) 'Panorama de un nuevo siglo. La literatura infantil en catalán'. *Bookbird*, 1, 1–5.

Nida, E. (1964) *Seminars on Translation and Culture*. Barcelona: Faculty of Translation and Interpreting, University of Vic.

Oficina de Justificación de la Difusión (2013) Online. www.ojd.es (accessed 23 July 2013).

Oittinen, R. (2000) *Translating for Children*. London and New York: Garland.

— (2003) 'Where the Wild Things Are: Translating picture books'. *Meta: Journal des traducteurs/Meta: Translators' Journal*, 48 (1), 128–41.

Oliva, S. (1995) 'Sobre els elements suposadament intraduïbles de la traducció literària'. In Marco, J. (ed.) *La traducció literària*. Castelló de la Plana: Universitat Jaume, 81–92.

— (1996) *Alícia al país de les meravelles*. Barcelona: Empúries.

— (1997) 'Pla ha guanyat Carner en el model de llengua'. *Avui*, 30 January, 4.

Parcerisas, F. (1997) 'Lo que se gana en traducción'. *Donaire*, 8, 54–9.

Pericay, X. and Toutain, F. (1996) *El malentès del Noucentisme: Tradició i plagi a la prosa catalana moderna*. Barcelona: Proa.

Pokorn, N.K. (2012) *Post-Socialist Translation Practices. Ideological struggle in children's literature*. Amsterdam: John Benjamins.

Rovira, T. and Ribé, C. (1972) *Bibliografía histórica del libro infantil en Catalán*. Madrid: Asociación Nacional de Bibliotecarios, Archiveros y Arqueólogos.

Shavit, Z. (2009) *Poetics of Children's Literature*. Originally 1986. Athens: University of Georgia Press.

Sorolla, N. (2012) 'Context demogràfic i econòmic. L'evolució de la comunitat lingüística'. In Xarxa Cruscat (ed.) *VI Informe sobre la situació de la llengua catalana*. Barcelona: Omnium Cultural i Plataforma per la llengua, 133–8.

Toury, G. (1995) 'The Nature and Role of Norms in Translation'. In Toury, G. (ed.) *Descriptive Translation Studies and Beyond*. Amsterdam: John Benjamins, 53–69.

Van Collie, J. and Verschueren, W.P. (eds) (2006) *Children's Literature in Translation: Challenges and Strategies*. Manchester: St Jerome.

Venuti, L. (1995) *The Translator's Invisibility: A history of translation*. London: Routledge.

Chapter 2

Windows between worlds
Loanwords in New Zealand children's picture books as an interface between two cultures
Nicola Daly

Introduction

Although *te reo Māori* (the Māori language) is the indigenous language of New Zealand, English is spoken by 95.9 per cent of the population (QuickStats about Culture and Identity, 2007), reflecting its British colonial history. In 1987 the Māori Language Act gave te reo Māori official language status and declared that te reo Māori could be used in all court proceedings, commissions of inquiry and tribunals. The Act created *Te Taura Whiri i Te Reo Māori*, the Māori Language Commission, whose central aim is to 'promote the use of Māori as a living language and as an ordinary means of communication' (Māori Language Commission, 2007).

By the 1950s, due mainly to urbanization and education, a generation of Māori had not learned to speak te reo Māori, and the language appeared to be heading towards decline (Macalister, 2005). This worrying trend led to the establishment in 1982 of the first *kōhanga reo* (Māori language preschools) and then in 1989 and 1990 to legislation for *kura kaupapa Māori* (Māori medium schools) and *wānanga* (universities). In 2013 16,792 students were receiving part or all of their education through the Māori language at schools throughout New Zealand (Māori Medium Education as at 1 July, 2013).

The English language is renowned for its capacity for borrowing and the growth in internationalism in recent times has, it is suggested, led people to seek new words to indicate their local identity (Crystal, 1995; Crystal, 2003). Certainly this is true of New Zealand English, most notably borrowing from te reo Māori (Deverson, 1991). In 1985 Deverson estimated that most New Zealanders have passive knowledge of at least 40 to 50 borrowed Māori loanwords (Deverson, 1985). This figure has been revised to 70 to 80 such words (Macalister, 2008). A study of the frequency of Māori loanwords in New Zealand English (NZE) in the *New Zealand School Journal* (an educational magazine publication) of the 1960s and 1990s showed an incidence of six words per 1,000 in both decades

(Macalister, 1999). Macalister (2006) has examined the use of Māori loanwords in New Zealand English across a 150-year period from 1850 to 2000. He examined a corpus of almost five and a half million words from three sources: newspapers, parliamentary debates and the *New Zealand School Journal*, and found an increase from 3.29 words per 1,000 in 1850 to 8.8 per 1,000 in 2000. Macalister explained this increase as due partly to the renaissance of Māori language and culture.

This chapter explores the use of Māori loanwords in New Zealand English using a corpus of picture books published in New Zealand between 1995 and 2005 to answer the following questions: (1) How is this quintessential aspect of New Zealand English reflected in children's picture books?; (2) What effect might this have on children's language acquisition?; (3) What factors influence authors' use of such loanwords? I argue that Māori loanwords in New Zealand English children's picture books may be seen as windows between worlds.

Frequency of loanwords

The first study examining the use of Māori loanwords in New Zealand English picture books was initiated when I became aware of the high use of such vocabulary in the picture books I was reading to my daughter. I wondered if there might in fact be a higher frequency than in other genres, and I speculated on the effect this would be having on the evolution of the New Zealand English dialect among children and adults reading these books.

I selected 13 picture books published between 1995 and 2005 by a New Zealand publisher specializing in Māori and Pasifika stories. The different kinds of loanwords ('types') in the picture books were identified and their numbers counted ('tokens') as a percentage of the total number of words in each book. The results showed 0.057, or 57 per 1,000 words, a much higher rate than in studies of other contexts. The highest frequency cited prior to this was 25 per 1,000 in a corpus of Hansard transcripts of a debate concerning Māori issues in the New Zealand parliament (Macalister, 2006). The considerably higher frequency found in the 13 picture books was possibly due to the fact that all of the authors were of Māori ethnicity, and because the publisher aimed to publish stories from a Māori perspective (Daly, 2007).

Whatever the reason for the higher frequency of loanwords, it is speculated that it will have an effect on the language use of New Zealand picture book readers and listeners, both young and old. The borrowed words may reflect the voices of some readers or listeners who already use loanwords, thus engaging that audience with the book and the words may increase the vocabulary of others who encounter loanwords for the first time in the context of the story. Cunningham (2005: 57) reviews several studies examining the effect of reading on children's vocabulary acquisition and concludes that 'overall the results suggest that shared book reading is an important and independent mechanism in the development of vocabulary in younger readers'.

Consequently I suggest that this higher frequency of loanwords in children's picture books has both a candle and mirror effect on a New Zealand dialect, and has educational implications. But are these picture books from a single publishing house representative of those published in New Zealand? To address this question, a second study examined almost all of the 500 picture books published in New Zealand in that same period (1995–2005).

The second study (Macdonald and Daly, 2013) involved analysing 469 English language picture books, 97 per cent of all those published in New Zealand between 1995 and 2005, to ascertain the frequency of Māori loanwords in each. The frequency varied from a low of 5 per 1,000 in 1997 to a high of 25 per 1,000 in 1999. The overall average frequency across the 11-year period was 13 per 1,000. Many books (n=315) used no loanwords at all, but if we examine only the books which did use loanwords (n=154) the mean frequency was 37 per 1,000, with a minimum of 16 per 1,000 in the year 2000, and a maximum of 52 per 1,000 in 1996, a rate more commensurate with my earlier study (Daly, 2007). Thus it appears that there may be two kinds of children's picture books available in New Zealand: those which use Māori loanwords, and use them quite frequently, and those which use none at all. The difference between these two kinds of books would be worth examining in more detail, but I hypothesize that whether loanwords are used in picture books depends on the author's ethnicity, the publisher's publishing focus, and the theme of the story in question.

Authors' decisions about using loanwords

The next study set out to examine in more detail the decision-making process of the authors who used Māori loanwords in their English texts, using as case studies two books which were available in both English and Māori versions: *Tekiteora, Kei Hea ō Hū?* (Gabel, 2003a) and its English language counterpart *Oh Hogwash, Sweet Pea!* (Gabel, 2003b); and *Koro's Medicine* (Drewery, 2004) and its Māori language version *Ngā rongoā a koro* (Drewery, 2005).

I used semi-structured interviews with the two authors and translators involved in the two picture books (Daly, 2008) and asked the authors about why they had chosen certain loanwords but not others. Their responses are discussed below.

Māori loanwords in English translation

Tekiteora, Kei Hea ō Hū? was first published in 2003 for the Ministry of Education, to be distributed in Māori medium preschools (*Ngā kōhanga reo*). The author wrote the book specifically to provide Māori language resources for bilingual children such as her daughter, and the illustrations include many items and images which belong to her family. About six months after its publication, the publishing company asked the author for permission for it to be translated for commercial release. The author agreed and worked closely with the translator on the translation.

Four Māori words remained in *Oh Hogwash, Sweet Pea!*, the English language version of *Tekiteora, Kei Hea ō Hū?*: *kūkupa, auē, Māmā* and *Pāpā. Kūkupa* is a Northern dialect word for the native wood pigeon, more commonly known as *kererū* in New Zealand English. This word was at first translated as 'native wood pigeon' but after much discussion the author made it clear that she felt it interfered with the flow or rhythm of the words in the story, and returned the word *kūkupa. Auē* which translates as 'Oh Dear!, a wail a cry or a bleat' (Ryan, 1997: 39) was left in the English version, according to the translator, because of the sound and because it is easy to understand the meaning. The author said she wanted to retain it as it maintains the original identity of the book and the sound fits well with the flow of words. In the context of the story, it is also easy to understand that it is an exclamation.

The use of these two vocabulary items (*kūkupa* and *auē*) in the English text reflects the importance of the sound of language in children's books, which are written to be read aloud and listened to. Lathey (2006: 10) sums this up: 'The aural texture of translation is of paramount importance to a child still engaged in discovering the power of language.'

Māmā and *Pāpā* are te reo Māori lexical items that exist in proto-Polynesian, and that differ from the English terms for parents in their use of long vowels (indicated by the macron) (Harlow, personal communication, 2007). Thus, despite their similarity to the English language equivalents, they are loanwords in the English text. They were retained in the English translation by the author of the original Māori text because she wanted her daughter's experience of using these names for her parents to be reflected in the book. The words were easy to understand and they maintained some cultural identity in the story. She made the point that many children in New Zealand call their parents by these names, but this is rarely reflected in literature or on television. She emphasized that she was not trying to make a political statement, but simply trying to maintain the integrity of her original story.

Māori loanwords in original English language text

Koro's Medicine (Drewery, 2004) was written by a Māori author who identified herself as a Māori language learner. She reported that she wrote this book with the intention to fill a gap in children's books about traditional Māori medicine. Before the English version of the book was published, the publisher asked one of their staff fluent in te reo Māori and familiar with traditional Māori medicine to translate it, and the two versions of the book were published one after another. Like *Tekiteora*, it has received many awards, including being listed in the White Raven Catalogue, an annually published list of internationally noteworthy books chosen by a panel at the International Youth Library, Germany, and named by IBBY (International Board on Books for Young People) as an outstanding book in promoting international understanding.

For *Koro's Medicine* the author reported that she deliberately used Māori loanwords for the native plants referred to in the story and that, as a Māori language learner herself, she tends to include words she is learning or has learnt in her writing. In this book she kept the focus on using loanwords relating to the subject of the book: *rongoā* ('Māori medicine'), but she also used words she considered to be in general usage such as *koro* ('grandpa'), *tama* ('son') and *whare* ('house'). So decisions around the use of many of the loanwords in this book reflected the language knowledge of the author and general loanword familiarity in NZE.

Rongoā ('Māori medicine') is not a commonly used loanword in NZE, but was obviously pivotal to this story of a grandfather teaching his grandson about Māori medicine. The advantage that borrowing words from another language offers is that distinctions can be made that otherwise may not be possible in the substrate language. When English borrowed large numbers of French words after the Norman invasion, for example, these borrowings allowed distinctions to be made between the animal *sheep* and the meat of the animal *mutton*. Likewise in the original English version of *Koro's Medicine*, using the word *rongoā* allows an easy distinction to be made between Māori medicine and other medicine:

'In the old days,' Koro said, 'there were no medicines in packets. Māori medicine came straight from the plants and trees. People shared their knowledge of rongoā with each other and passed it down through the generations.'

(Drewery, 2004: n.p.)

Words changed to English

Several words in the original Māori version of *Tekiteora, Kei Hea ō Hū?* (Gabel, 2003a) could have been left in Māori in the English version but were not; for example, *waka*. While *waka* is sometimes used in NZE (Macalister, 2005: 152), the translator decided to use 'canoes' because *waka* can also mean 'car'.

Another word which caused intense discussion and deliberation within the publishing team of *Oh Hogwash, Sweet Pea!* was the word *ehara*. This exclamation, which Ryan translates as 'Look at that!' or 'Lo and behold!' (1997: 42) and which in many Māori dialects suggests 'I doubt it' or 'I don't think so' (Rau, personal communication, 2007), is repeated often by the father in the story when he discovers his daughter's shoes in rather ordinary locations such as the laundry or the car.

Given that *ehara* is an exclamation similar to *auē*, which was left in, I asked the translator if she had considered leaving the original word *ehara* in the English text. She replied that this had never been considered, as it was a less familiar exclamation than *auē* and 'given that the story hangs on this piece of dialogue [i.e. *Hogwash*], I think it [*ehara*] would have rendered the English version inaccessible and somewhat weak as a story'.

The translator strongly believed that an interesting word such as *humbug* or *hogwash* should be used in the place of *ehara* because 'you can put any word in a kids' book and they will learn it and it's really good for them'. She explained that this is why she used words such as *epiphany* and *conundrum* in a book she later wrote herself. She said, 'I definitely think the kids need to be given exciting words, interesting words, not just "No way!" and "Yeah, right!"', which were other possible translations of *ehara*. Her answer indicates the complexity of decision making when translating. On the one hand the translator values introducing children to new and exciting vocabulary, but on the other hand she is aware of the big picture, and her overall aim is to make the story work for the child.

Both stories examined in this third study were written with educative motives: one author wished to introduce her daughter and other speakers of Māori to specific linguistic structures; the other author wished to introduce Māori medicine to English-speaking children. Thus we see several factors that influence the use of Māori loanwords: dialectal influences; the sound and rhythm of words; staying true to the original context of a story; the familiarity of loanwords in New Zealand English; the relevance of the loanword to the topic of the story; the potential for ambiguity; and the importance of the word to the integrity of the story. These considerations can be aligned with Toury's (1995) norms of translation. Dialectal considerations, original context and integrity of the story relate to 'adequacy' in terms of adhering to the norms of the source language, whereas the sounds and rhythm of words, familiarity of loanwords and the potential for ambiguity are an indication of the translation being 'acceptable' in terms of the target language norms. It is apparent that in many cases the loanwords provide a window between worlds. The author of *Oh Hogwash, Sweet Pea!* wanted to retain *Māmā* and *Pāpā* because this is what her daughter, like many Māori children, calls her parents; she used *kūkupa* because this is the name of a bird in the dialect of Māori she speaks. The author of *Koro's Medicine* chose words she thought were familiar to most New Zealand readers – windows which had already been opened for many readers. But she also chose words which she was learning as a Māori language learner – windows that for her and perhaps for her readers were opened by reading the story.

Effects of loanwords on cultural knowledge

But what effect do these words in these texts have on those who are reading them? This question led to the fourth study reported in this chapter. This examined how a group of ten families responded to a set of New Zealand English picture books which used a high frequency of loanwords.

The fourth study (Daly, 2009; Daly, 2010) involved ten non-Māori parents (nine female and one male aged between 34 and 41 years) who took home the collection of 13 NZE picture books published between 1995 and 2005 mentioned above to read to their children (aged between 1 and 7 years) over a month. They were instructed to incorporate the books into their normal story reading time, and to follow their children's interests in terms of which books to read and how often. After the month I interviewed the parents about their children's and their own responses to the stories.

The participants all reported that reading the books had an effect on their own and sometimes on their children's language use. In the initial set of six questions regarding familiarity with te reo Māori, Anne (pseudonyms are used) reported that her family sang *waiata* (songs) every day at home, and that she used occasional loanwords such as *kai* (food) and *puku* (tummy). Anne reported that she was actively trying to use more Māori words in her spoken English after reading the books. She reported using *Tangaroa* (the god of the sea) at the beach, and *aniwaniwa* (rainbow) when her son drew a picture of a rainbow. She told me that while her children did not actually use more loanwords themselves they seemed to understand more when she used them.

Brian and Carol were the parents of two children. Prior to reading the books both reported using loanwords more around their children than in any other context, including words such as *haka* (war dance) and *piwakawaka* (fantail bird). Carol said she used more loanwords around her children than with adults because she was uncertain of her pronunciation and thus afraid of making a mistake. Also she worked with many Māori students and used the loanwords with them. Her husband reported using several relevant loanwords when at work and using more loanwords himself after reading the books with his daughter, such as *aniwaniwa* (rainbow), *tumeke* (great), *ti kauka* (cabbage tree) and *kūkupa* (native wood pigeon). His wife reported that she was more familiar with the words after reading the books, but remained less confident about their use and production. Both Brian and Carol thought their daughter understood more loanwords as a result of reading the books, but had not witnessed her producing them.

Before she read the books to her son for this study, Debbie, who had just completed a year's course in te reo Māori, reported using more loanwords when speaking English in the context of her course, but also when speaking with people who used many loanwords. After reading the books for this research she reported no effect on her language use as she was already using a lot of Māori loanwords, but said that reading the books made her want more loanwords: 'I did feel like, Oh no, I could have books with more Māori words in them.' Thus for Debbie the use of loanwords was linked to her own developing bilingualism. She also noticed that although her son was not using noticeably more loanwords, he was asking for more Māori songs to be played, and she believed that he now chose more books with loanwords from the library. So there was a sense in which the presence of this set of books in the house normalized books using loanwords.

Erin reported that prior to reading the books for this study she had tried to use loanwords at home because one of her family has Māori heritage. After reading the books she reported using the word *taniwha* ('monster') and learning Māori names for birds from *Roimata's Cloak* (Tamehana, 1997). Reading the books reminded her to use te reo Māori more frequently with her children. Fiona initially reported that she believed that there was no effect on her use of loanwords from reading the books, but then she remembered that she had used *taniwha* to mean 'monster' and so had her son. Both Erin's and Fiona's usage of *taniwha* came directly from the book *Taming the Taniwha* (Tipene, 2001), which tells the story of a young boy

(Tama) dealing with a bully at school, who is labelled a '*taniwha*' by the people in his family to whom he goes for advice.

All ten adult reader participants reported that reading these books to their children had affected their own knowledge of *tikanga Māori* (Māori culture). Anne said she had learnt about the traditional Māori fishing practice of giving the first catch to *Tangaroa* (from *Timo and the Kingfish*, Reedy, 2000), about the legend of *Whirikoki* (in *Whirikoki and his Seal*, Clarke, 1997) and about the practice of extended family coming together around birth and death (from *Haere*, Tipene, 2005). Brian had learnt more about Māori medicine or *rongoā* from *Koro's Medicine* (Drewery, 2004) and the formality of speeches and *waiata* (songs) from *Haere* (Tipene, 2005). Carol commented on the reflection of contemporary Māori culture in the Cuzzies books (Kapai, 2004a; Kapai, 2004b), which had given her insights into the lives of some of the children she works with. Erin reported no specific new knowledge regarding *tikanga Māori*, but that she felt she was building on knowledge she already had. Fiona reported learning more about Māori medicine (from *Koro's Medicine*), about *Tangaroa* and the traditional Māori practice of returning the first catch to the sea (from *Timo and the Kingfish*).

Clearly this set of NZE picture books, incorporating so many Māori loanwords, did provide a window into another world for the non-Māori parents, who all reported some effect on their own or their children's language or cultural knowledge. It is likely that the same would happen in the classroom.

Pedagogical implications

The use of Māori loanwords in New Zealand picture books provides many potential pedagogical affordances for multilingual and multicultural classrooms. For the children and adult readers who use many loanwords in their spoken NZE, the use of loanwords in these books acts to validate their identity. Readers are 'hearing' their own voices in the stories. In their discussion of multicultural literature for children Galda and Callinan write: 'If children never see themselves in books, that omission subtly tells these young people that they are not important enough to appear in books, that books are not for them' (2002: 277). Thus the use of loanwords in children's picture books could act as a subtly powerful validation of the voice of such readers and listeners. One adult participant in a related study in which she read a set of 13 books to her son over a month commented that she felt she was being immersed in her own culture (Daly, 2010).

For the children and parents who do not use many loanwords, reading these books may act to increase their use of loanwords in their spoken NZE.

The studies described have shown that reading books with a high frequency of loanwords did affect the reported spoken language of parent readers. Cunningham (2005) has reviewed many studies of adults reading books to children that show that, after even one reading, children can pick up new vocabulary from the books they hear.

But is the increased use of Māori loanwords in New Zealand English desirable? In his overview of the place of te reo Māori in Aotearoa/New Zealand, Benton (2007) discusses the special place of this language in the New Zealand national identity. This echoes the earlier observation by Deverson (1991) that the use of loanwords in NZE is one of its most distinctive characteristics. Because of this special and strong link between Māori loanwords and NZE and the New Zealand national identity, the use of Māori loanwords in NZE picture books has the potential to contribute to the growth of a distinctive New Zealand linguistic identity. If such books are used in classrooms both readers and listeners will become familiar with the Māori words and concepts featured in the stories. This relationship between children's literature and national identity is extensively explored in other contexts, including the Canadian (Bainbridge, 2002; Bainbridge and Wolodko, 2002; Desai, 2006; Williams, 2001). In her study of the ways in which Canadian children's literature can be used to influence Canadian children's sense of national identity, Bainbridge notes that '[l]iterature is a powerful vehicle for the transmission of national culture and national identity' (2002: 66). In this case the New Zealand national identity being transmitted is, by virtue of the Māori concepts and words being used, more diverse and inclusive.

Conclusion

The four studies described in this chapter have explored the significant presence of loanwords in New Zealand. As Macalister (2005) suggests, they may reflect the renaissance of the Māori language in New Zealand. It appears that Māori loanwords are used in picture books with higher frequency than in other domains that have been examined (Macalister, 1999; Macalister, 2006). This may be because the picture book provides images to accompany unfamiliar vocabulary. It may also reflect the ethnicity of authors, and the frequency of loanwords in their own NZE idiolects. The findings also point to the pedagogical potential of such picture books in classrooms to reflect the identity of some readers and listeners, and expand the perspective of others, thus creating windows between worlds.

References

Bainbridge, J.M. (2002) 'The role of Canadian children's literature in national identity formation'. *English Quarterly*, 34 (3–4), 166–74.

Bainbridge, J.M. and Wolodko, B. (2002) 'Canadian picture books: Shaping and reflecting national identity'. *Bookbird*, 40 (2), 21–7.

Benton, R. (2007). 'Mauri or mirage? The status of the Maori language in Aotearoa New Zealand in the third millennium'. In Tsui, A.B.M. and Tollefson, J.W. (eds) *Language Policy, Culture and Identity in Asian Contexts*. Mahwah, NJ: Lawrence Erlbaum, 163–81.

Clarke, M. (1997) *Whirikoki and his Seal*. Wellington: Huia Publishers.

Crystal, D. (1995) *The Cambridge Encyclopedia of the English Language*. Cambridge: Cambridge University Press.

— (2003) *A Dictionary of Linguistics and Phonetics*. 5th edn. Maldon, MA: Blackwell Publishing.

Cunningham, A.E. (2005) 'Vocabulary growth through independent reading and reading aloud to children'. In Hiebert, E.H. and Kamil, M.L. (eds) *Teaching and Learning Vocabulary: Bringing research to practice*. Mahwah, NJ: Lawrence Erlbaum, 45–68.

Daly, N. (2007) 'Kūkupa, koro, and kai: The use of Māori vocabulary items in New Zealand English children's picture books'. *The New Zealand English Journal*, 21, 20–33.

— (2008) 'The narrative contract and the use of Māori loanwords in New Zealand English picture books'. *Journal of Children's Literature Studies*, 5 (2), 1–17.

— (2009) 'Overhearing Tangi, Tangaroa, and Taniwha: The reported effects of Māori loanwords in children's picture books on language use and cultural knowledge of adult readers'. *Te Reo*, 52, 3–16.

— (2010) '"Right here, right now": Embracing New Zealand national identity through the Māori loanwords used in New Zealand English children's picture books'. *Journal of Children's Literature Studies*, 7 (2), 22–37.

Desai, C. (2006) 'National identity in a multicultural society: Malaysian children's literature in English'. *Children's Literature in Education*, 37 (2), 163–84.

Deverson, T. (1985) '"Home loans": Māori input into current New Zealand English'. *English in New Zealand*, 33, 4–10.

— (1991) 'New Zealand lexis: The Māori dimension'. *English Today*, 7 (2), 18–25.

Drewery, M. (2004) *Koro's Medicine*. Wellington: Huia Publishers.

— (2005) *Ngä rongoä a koro*. Trans. Uatuku, K. Wellington: Huia Publishers.

Gabel, N. (2003a) *Tekiteora, Kei Hea ö Hü?* Trans. Rainsforth, H. Wellington: Huia Publishers.

— (2003b) *Oh Hogwash, Sweet Pea!* Wellington: Huia Publishers.

Galda, L. and Callinan, B.E. (2002) *Cullinan and Galda's Literature and the Child*. Belmont, CA: Wadsworth/Thomson Learning.

Ihimaera, W. (2002) *The Little Kowhai Tree*. Wellington: Huia Publishers.

Kapai, T. (2004a) *Cuzzies find the Rainbow's End*. Wellington: Huia Publishers.

— (2004b) *Cuzzies meet the Motuhoa Shark*. Wellington: Huia Publishers.

Kennedy, G. and Yamazaki, S. (1999) 'The influence of Māori on the New Zealand English lexicon'. In Kirk, J.M. (ed.) *Corpora Galore: Analyses and techniques in describing English*. Amsterdam: Rodopi, 33–44.

Lathey, G. (2006) 'Time, narrative intimacy and the child: Implications of tense switching in the translation of picture books in English'. In Lathey, G. (ed.) *The Translation of Children's Literature: A reader*. Clevedon: Multilingual Matters, 134–41.

Macalister, J. (1999) 'Trends in New Zealand English: Some observations on the presence of Māori words in the lexicon'. *New Zealand English Journal*, 13, 38–49.

— (2005) *A Dictionary of Māori Words in New Zealand English*. Melbourne: Oxford University Press.

— (2006) 'The Māori presence in the New Zealand English lexicon, 1850–2000'. *English World-Wide*, 27 (1), 1–24.

— (2008) 'Tracking changes in familiarity with borrowings from te reo Māori'. *Te Reo*, 51, 75–97.

MacDonald, D. and Daly, N. (2013) 'Kiwi, kapai, and kuia: Māori loanwords in New Zealand English children's picture books published between 1995 and 2005'. In Carrington, B. and Pinsent, P. (eds) *The Final Chapters: Concluding papers of the Journal of Children's Literature Studies*. Wizard's Tower Press, 44–56.

Māori Language Commission (2007) 'About us: What is the Māori Language Commission'. Online. www.tetaurawhiri.govt.nz/english/about_e (accessed 20 August 2007).

Māori Medium Education as at 1 July (2013) Online. www.educationcounts.govt. nz/statistics/maori_education/schooling/6040 (accessed 30 July 2013).

Mataira, K.T.H. (1998) *Rangi and his Dinosaurs*. Wellington: Huia Publishers.

QuickStats about Culture and Identity (2007) Online. www.stats.govt.nz/ Census/2006CensusHomePage/QuickStats/quickstats-about-a-subject/culture-and-identity.aspx (accessed 10 June 2014).

Reedy, M.P. (2000) *Timo and the Kingfish*. Wellington: Huia Publishers.

Ryan, P.M. (1997) *The Reed Dictionary of Modern Māori*. Auckland: Reed Publishing.

Tamehana, E. (1997) *The Sandman*. Wellington: Huia Publishers.

— (2005) *Roimata's Cloak*. Wellington: Huia Publishers.

Tawhara, M. (2000) *The Pūriri Tree*. Wellington: Huia Publishers.

Tipene, T. (2001) *Taming the Taniwha*. Wellington: Huia Publishers.

— (2005) *Haere*. Wellington: Huia Publishers.

Toury, G. (1995) *Descriptive Translation Studies and Beyond*. Amsterdam and New York: John Benjamins.

Williams, S. (2001) 'The Czech Republic: The creation of national identity: Significance of Jan Karafiat's Broucci to Czech children's literature'. *Bookbird*, 39 (1), 46–51.

Chapter 3

Translating heritage languages

Promoting intercultural and plurilingual competences through children's literature

Caterina Sugranyes Ernest and Maria González Davies

Introduction

This chapter focuses on the need to foster plurilingual and intercultural competences in schools and to develop educational and language policies in recognition of the increasingly plural society. Despite the large body of research confirming the importance of building on previously acquired linguistic knowledge in learning other languages (Cook, 2001; Cook, 2010; Corcoll, 2012; Cummins, 2007; González Davies, 2012; Herdina and Jessner, 2002), the teaching and learning of languages in Catalonia is still very much based on a monolingual paradigm where existing languages are excluded from the target language class (Corcoll, 2012; Goitia and Sugranyes, 2011). A plurilingual approach to language teaching would not only help to deal with the challenges embedded in a plural society, but also help newly arrived pupils to integrate in school by using their family languages as meaningful tools for learning other languages.

In this study we use the term 'heritage languages', defined as the languages associated with a person's cultural background (Cho, 2000), to refer to the languages pupils newly arrived in the country bring to the classroom. In many classrooms the focus is on ensuring that newly arrived pupils are assimilated within the receiving culture (Cummins, 2005; Escobar and Unamuno, 2008; Vila, 2005), rather than valuing the importance of cultural heritage in enabling them to interact effectively across different languages and cultures.

Within a plurilingual approach, translation is a pedagogical tool for learning languages and for acquiring mediation skills (Cummins, 2007; González Davies, 2011; González Davies, 2012; González Davies, forthcoming) where two or more cultural realities interact. Moreover, literary translation can involve a plurality of interpretations and conceptualizations of the world, which, as in this study, are mapped on to the stories that are written and translated by the children themselves. Such stories can be an ideal tool for promoting both language and cultural awareness.

In contrast to the common practice of banning translation and the use of the heritage languages in the language classroom, the study presented here demonstrates how the translation of children's literature can be highly beneficial in a context where heritage languages coexist. We argue that translation can be used to promote intercultural and plurilingual competences among pupils, as the heritage of each child-author is highlighted through the stories they create.

Catalonia: Language diversity and language use

During the Spanish dictatorship of General Franco (1939–1975), Catalan was outlawed from education and public life in general and so was relegated only to family and social use. In the post-Franco period Catalan again became the official language of Catalonia together with Spanish. To deal with the challenges of the coexistence of two languages, the *Programa d'Imersió Lingüística*, an immersion system based on Cummins's Linguistic Interdependency Hypothesis (1979), was implemented in 1983. It aimed to promote Catalan as the language of instruction among all students, and resulted in a language shift for many children, who spoke Spanish at home and Catalan at school.

A new linguistic and ethnic scenario has now emerged in Catalonia. The number of inhabitants originating from other countries has increased by nearly 20 per cent in the last ten years (IDESCAT, 2013). They represent 170 nationalities and speak 200 different languages. It could be that the immersion approach is no longer appropriate within the bilingual context on which the Catalan education system is based. In Hélot's words: 'bilingual programmes do not cater for the plurilingual repertoire of all learners' (2011: 43). Groups that are linguistically heterogeneous are now a reality in many schools in Catalonia (Serra Bonet, 2010). There is a need for newly arrived pupils to understand and speak Catalan as quickly as possible, hence the language immersion programmes (Vila, 2005). But, as Cummins puts it, 'we are faced with the bizarre scenario of schools successfully transforming fluent speakers of foreign languages into monolingual speakers' (2005: 586). Moreover, schools with large numbers of newly arrived pupils are often stigmatized as they are believed to be attaining lower academic results than schools with few such children.

Drawing on research developed by Cummins (2005), Cook (2007), González Davies (forthcoming), Guasch (2010), Herdina and Jessner (2002) and Vila (2005), we will argue that instead of regarding the presence of newly arrived children in the classroom as an impediment for overall academic performance in Catalonia, pupils' heritage language proficiency should be viewed as a useful resource for learning other languages (Cummins, 2005). Using all languages actively in both language- and content-based subjects, that is, adopting a plurilingual approach to teaching and learning, can greatly enhance language learning in general, and translation has a crucial role in these contexts as an effective and necessary learning and teaching tool.

Foreign language learning in primary education in Catalonia

English is studied as a third language in Catalonia, officially starting at the age of 8, although many schools begin even earlier. As a result of the general concern that the level of English remains very low when students finish their secondary education, the Catalan government initiated the *Pla d'impúls de les terceres llengües* – the plan for the development of third languages (May 2007). This aims to train teachers to teach content subjects in English – Content Language Integrated Learning (CLIL) – at all levels and also to develop new strategies to improve language teaching in general. In spite of this policy, there are still great differences between what the government requires and actual classroom practice: the teachers' level of English is still very low and many have not been trained to teach content subjects in English.

Moreover, in many schools with high numbers of newly arrived pupils, English is considered to be the least important subject. Learning Catalan and Spanish is considered to be difficult enough and English is seen as a problem. The underlying assumption is that these newcomers will not be able to cope with so many languages. Pupils who are identified as needing to spend time in special reception classes for new arrivals in which 'core subjects' are taught are frequently withdrawn from English classes, as these are deemed less important (Escobar and Unamuno, 2008).

Based on data collected during a two-month observation period in the school where we conducted this study, it seems that pupils feel especially motivated in the foreign language class (Goitia and Sugranyes, 2011), precisely because it is the foreign language classroom, and most pupils – if not all – share the same feeling of 'foreign-ness' towards the new language. Thus, for those pupils whose heritage language is not Spanish or Catalan, English could be conceived as a more equalizing means of communication than Catalan or Spanish. The English classroom could therefore be seen as an excellent context in which to work towards language and content improvement, as pupils seem to feel more at ease and comfortable here than in other academic settings.

From the monolingual to the plurilingual paradigm

The monolingual immersion paradigm decreed in 1983, as practised in Catalan schools, is not supported by recent research into language acquisition. The research shows that previously acquired knowledge is valuable knowledge that should be taken into account in the learning process (Aronin and Singleton, 2012; González Davies, forthcoming) and that using the learners' knowledge of the heritage language significantly helps them to learn other languages (Cummins, 2005). The monolingual paradigm is also inimical to recent research into how the bilingual and multilingual mind works (Herdina and Jessner, 2002; Cook, 2007). As stated in the Plurilingual Development Paradigm (González Davies, forthcoming), plurilingualism relates to the fact that an individual's experience of language in its cultural contexts expands from the language of the home to that of society at large and then to the languages of other people.

The plurilingual approach to language learning derives from recent research that follows Cummins's Common Underlying Proficiency Model Hypothesis. This proposes that individuals have different underlying skills that make connections between languages and cultures possible (Cummins, 1984). The dynamic model of multilingualism (Herdina and Jessner, 2002) focuses on the link between the sociolinguistic and psycholinguistic variations present in multilingual systems. Cook's definition of multicompetence as the knowledge of two or more languages in one mind (2001) explores 'how bi- and plurilinguals think and learn differently from monolinguals and acquire additional skills and know-how that are not purely linguistic but are related to successful (language) learning' (González Davies, forthcoming).

Guasch's research on the integration of plurilingual strategies in schools (2010) also supports the view that the teaching of languages in school is best approached in an integrated manner. Yet language departments for Catalan, Spanish and English in many Catalonian schools are quite separate and there is no integration of pedagogy for all three languages.

Extensive research shows that bilingual and plurilingual pupils are at a great advantage when learning languages, as compared to monolingual speakers (cf. Baker, 2011; Bialystok, 2001; Cenoz and Genesse, 1998; Clyne, 2003). In line with Cook's (2001) multicompetence theory, by moving towards a more plurilingual approach to language teaching, and arguably also through the pupils' experience and conceptualization of the world through their own heritage, their intercultural competence, as well as their languages, would be made visible and this would be likely to lead to overall academic improvement. These views are supported by Cho (2000), who showed that those pupils who have developed and maintained proficiency in their heritage language have greater understanding and knowledge of different cultures and ethics and are also better able to mediate between cultures.

National and international language policies also state the need for a change in paradigm: the Common European Framework for Languages states the need to meet the demands of a 'highly multilingual and multicultural Europe' (CEFRL, 2001: 3) through language learning in order to create 'plurilingual speakers who act as linguistic and cultural intermediaries and mediators' (CEFRL, 2001: 9). Speakers no longer aspire simply to become like native speakers of the additional language, but aim towards becoming intercultural speakers whose proficiency enables them to communicate and to share knowledge with others (Alcón, 2007). The objective of the Language Area of the Catalan Curriculum for Primary Education is 'to prepare students who live in Catalonia ... to be able to face the challenges of the plural, multilingual and multicultural society' (CCPE, 2009: 30).

Although national and international language policies are not always as effective in the classroom as intended, there does seem to be an overall recognition of the need to move towards a more plurilingual approach. There are a great many initiatives and good practices that aim to deal with issues related to linguistic and cultural diversity in schools in Catalonia and elsewhere. One example is a website that offers a wide range of good practices, aimed at helping to develop this diversity (www.xtec.cat/web/ projectes/alumnatnou).

The use of translation in the foreign language classroom

Research on the use of translation as an effective tool for additional language learning is relatively recent (Cook, 2010; Corcoll, 2012; González Davies, 2011; González Davies, 2012; González Davies, forthcoming; Leonardi, 2012). Language learning has long been based on the assumption that the target language had to be used exclusively in the language classroom without referring to the student's first language and that translation should be banned (Richards and Rodgers, 2001). Translation can, however, be considered as an opportunity to highlight heritage languages and this is especially relevant when these languages are not prioritized in the environment in which these speakers live, as in the case of Catalonia. Translation also plays an important role in enabling mono-, bilingual and newly arrived pupils to participate actively in instruction (Cummins, 2007). Within a plurilingual approach to language teaching, adopting 'translation to acquire linguistic mediation skills and intercultural competence in fields other than translation studies (TOLC)' (González Davies, 2012) is relevant to this study as an informed use of translation promotes intercultural and plurilingual competences as linguistic skills are acquired.

Literary translation is an intercultural experience (Hélot and O'Laoire, 2011). A plural approach to children's literature through translation can also promote plurilingual and intercultural competences among pupils as a means of encouraging language visibility, use and awareness, and of improving additional language skills. Recent research proves the positive outcomes of using the translation of children's literature in the classroom as a way to improve intercultural communication competence (Goitia and Sugranyes, 2011; González Davies, 2011; González Davies, 2012; Hélot, 2011). Encouraging the love of reading and writing in a relaxed learning atmosphere may also improve reading and writing skills and attitudes towards languages. The use of translation in a plurilingual primary school context can be considered an opportunity for children recently settled in a new country to value and to express themselves in their own language. Translating from English into Tagalog or Urdu entails 'promoting' these languages to the same level as English, making them visible to others. It creates a legitimate space for multilingual students to demonstrate their expertise. The teacher may not know the languages being used in the classroom, but the class will have interpreters/translators who can facilitate understanding and learning, and the children feel that their culture and their language are supported.

The study

The study presents an ecological perspective on language teaching: all languages are seen as meaningful resources, both for those who already speak them and for those who do not. An exploratory pilot study was designed over a four-month period and three research questions were formulated. Can a plurilingual approach to additional language teaching through translation and children's literature:

a) Contribute to the improvement of academic performance of all academic languages within the class as a whole?
b) Improve pupils' motivation and attitudes towards learning languages?
c) Increase intercultural communicative competence?

The research paradigm followed was quasi-experimental, interpretative and socio-critical. Quantitative data were collected by using the following pre- and post-tests:

- the mini Attitude and Motivation Battery Test – AMBT – (Bernaus and Gardner, 2008) in order to assess degrees of motivation and attitudes towards language learning
- the Intercultural Communication Competence Test (Baños, 2003) in order to assess levels of intercultural communication competence
- marks for Catalan, English and Spanish in order to assess academic performance in these languages.

The main researcher and the class teacher gathered qualitative data through personal interviews, observation sheets, researcher's diary, teacher's diary and recordings. These were analysed and used comparatively in order to triangulate the results.

Context and participants

The study was carried out in a sixth-year classroom with pupils from a state primary school in the Raval neighbourhood in the centre of Barcelona. The class consisted of 19 children aged 11 and 12. Only two pupils were born in Spain; the other 17 had been living in Catalonia for different lengths of time (from one to ten years). Nine pupils spoke two or more languages at home other than Catalan or Spanish (primarily Tagalog-Ilokano or Urdu-Panjabi). Four pupils spoke one language at home other than Spanish or Catalan (Chinese, Arabic, Bangla) and the rest spoke Spanish at home.

Within the school, the concept of cultural diversity is highly valued: examples of different words in the different languages spoken by pupils ('good morning', 'happy birthday', 'welcome', etc.) are displayed on the corridor walls. Contact with families is also constant and, from a very early age, pupils become interpreters between the school and their families. There is a clear sensitivity towards cultural and linguistic diversity, yet it is never used in the classrooms for teaching purposes.

Catalan is the main language in the school and all the teachers and staff speak it to all the pupils. All subjects are taught in Catalan except for Spanish lessons and English lessons. Nevertheless, the pupils' Catalan is poor or non-existent. Some pupils arrive at the school without speaking any Catalan or Spanish. The main linguistic goal of the school is that Catalan should not be used only for academic purposes. The reality is totally different: pupils only speak Catalan to teachers when they transmit a message given by a teacher or when they are taking part in an activity in class. As in many schools, the language departments each function independently.

Pupils have five hours of English language lessons a week. The overall level of English of the class is not very high. A few pupils do have a good command of English, especially those from Pakistan, Bangladesh and the Philippines. Even though the teacher uses Catalan in order to explain unclear concepts and to translate words that are not understood in the English language class, Catalan is regarded as a tool through which students understand English and no other languages are used or referred to in the class.

The storybook project: Creating stories in different languages

Pupils were told they would have to create their own stories in English, translate them into their heritage language with the help of their families and then read them to younger children (aged 3 to 5) on Saint George's Day on 23 April. It is traditional to give books and roses to loved ones on that day, *la Diada de Sant Jordi*. The stories would be placed in the school library for other pupils to read. The children worked in groups of four according to heritage language, foreign language competence and general academic performance. The project had five phases.

Phase I: Reading
Pupils were read three English language books: *Brown Bear, Brown Bear, What do you See?* (Martin, 2007); *The Very Hungry Caterpillar* (Carle, 1969); and *Where's Spot?* (Hill, 1983). The overall level of English of the class was quite low so it was appropriate to start with books that were easy to comprehend. The initial book reading was intended as a brainstorming activity to draw attention to language, format and content, as it made pupils aware of vocabulary used, simple structures and format.

Phase II: Writing stories
Pupils had to follow a specific format (eight to ten pages with one or two sentences per page), defining characters, plot and illustrations.

Phase III: Translating stories
Following Hervey, Higgins and Haywood's suggested degrees of fidelity in translation (1995: 13–14) and using simple examples, communicative versus literal translations were discussed. The pupils were asked to translate their English language stories into their heritage languages. They were encouraged to help each other and to seek help at home. Language games

such as silent dictations or bilingual readings were introduced to promote language awareness and make pupils use the different languages in a significant manner. Finally, the children illustrated their texts and prepared the final versions of the books.

Phase IV: Storytelling

Pupils practised storytelling in the classroom, first in groups and then in front of the class, and peer assessment was encouraged. They were asked to fill in a grid with the following items:

- clarity of speech
- speed
- pronunciation
- non-verbal communication.

Phase V: Saint George's Day

The pupils read their stories to the younger children in English and in all the heritage languages. During the festivities of *la Diada de Sant Jordi* pupils from the infants came to the auditorium to hear the stories written by older children in their heritage languages.

Results and discussion

Effect of the project on pupils' overall language proficiency

After the storybook project ended, the pupils' language results were compared to the marks they had obtained at the start of the term. A simple statistical data analysis revealed a significant improvement in the children's academic performance in all three school languages: 34 per cent of pupils obtained higher marks in the three languages than in the earlier assessment. These results support the research in bilingual and multilingual acquisition and the positive effects on language learning (Cenoz and Valencia, 1994; Lasagabaster, 1997) referred to in this study. The marks for Spanish of 31 per cent of pupils who spoke Spanish at home also improved, confirming that knowing a second language benefits the use of the first language (Cook, 2003; Corcoll, 2012).

Effect of the project on pupils' motivation and attitudes towards languages

A t-Test analysis of the results of the Attitude and Motivation Battery Test suggests that motivation for learning language increased significantly (p=0.02). Specifically, a substantial change in the instrumental orientation towards English was noted. It appears that participants could see that using English significantly, by translating from English into their heritage languages, helped them to enhance their own languages.

A slight increase in motivation for learning Spanish and English was noted in the pupils who spoke Spanish at home. This could be because their own language is used, alongside all the others, in an academic context other than just in the Spanish class. Also relevant is the effect on pupils who spoke only Spanish at home of the negative response towards using it in and outside school, given the emphasis on Catalan at school and in society. This may diminish their interest in learning languages.

Thanks to the project, pupils' attitudes towards learning languages improved significantly ($p=0.02$). This could be because they were now able to see the importance of using languages in an academic context in a meaningful way. It could also be that making heritage languages visible in an academic context made them want to learn other academic languages (see Cho, 2000).

A qualitative account of several stages of the project shows how pupils' attitudes towards languages developed. Their initial response to the proposal was telling:

> 'What language will I translate into if I speak Spanish?'
> 'And if I speak two languages at home, which one should I choose?'
> 'I know how to speak Urdu but I don't know to write it.'
>> (Extracts taken from recordings, January 2009, our translation. Due to limitations of space we have included only the translation)

Already we can see how, at the early stage of implementing the project, metalinguistic awareness was being promoted, as pupils spontaneously reached their own conclusions as to what the process of translation involved and expressed their plurilingualism unconsciously and naturally.

Grouping pupils according to language proved to be an interesting and thought-provoking task. They had never been grouped according to the language they spoke at home. It had never occurred to them that the fact that nine different languages coexisted in a classroom of only 19 pupils was interesting in itself. The idea of sharing this with the rest of the school through the stories they had created seemed to them innovative and exciting.

The writing process involved in developing the plot of each story was much more complex than expected, presumably due to the pupils' low level of English. They were not used to free writing in English, and despite the teacher's clear instructions that the books were intended for younger children so vocabulary and language structures had to be easy, the whole process became somewhat difficult. For similar tasks in the future, it was clear that pupils would benefit from being given more detailed guidance both during the initial design of the plot and the subsequent writing of the text (e.g. using vocabulary mind maps and clearer outlines). And it would have been useful to have asked pupils to bring books written in their own languages to class, as a boost to language sensitivity and awareness.

The class dynamics changed radically once pupils started using their own languages to translate the texts written in English. Speaking and using their own language in the classroom boosted their confidence: they felt important, singled out and valued. As can be seen from this extract taken from the teacher's diary (March 2009), two pupils who normally felt too embarrassed to speak in English started to do so: 'Pupil X never says much in class, and now he has started to participate, to give his opinion.' When they saw that their language and culture were supported and respected, the pupils clearly felt more at ease in the classroom. The attitudes of the Spanish-speaking pupils towards English also improved: before, 'They were embarrassed to speak in English, because they knew their English was worse than the Filipino and the Pakistani pupils' English' (Teacher's diary, May 2009).

The different languages unfolded through translation games and exercises. They stopped being static unknown linguistic codes and became useful tools from which the pupils could learn and through which they could discover that different languages have many more similarities than differences. Using translation and using their own languages developed their metalinguistic awareness. As one child observed: 'The past tense is much easier in English than in Spanish isn't it?'

On Saint George's Day 12 different languages were spoken in the school auditorium and most, if not all, the pupils heard their own language being read aloud. The younger children stared in disbelief as they heard their own language being spoken in school. Books in the relevant languages were exhibited during the week, and parents and families were encouraged to come and read and enjoy their children's work.

The effect of the project on pupils' levels of intercultural competence

It was apparent from the qualitative data extracted from the researcher's observation sheet that whereas all pupils were aware of the differences in how their peers did things (when working in groups, for example, a Chinese pupil was troubled when anyone sat too close to him and 'invaded his space'), at times the children failed to respect these differences and even made fun of them. An analysis of the Intercultural Competence Test concluded that the level of intercultural competence increased by only 1 per cent. A more sustained intervention along with activities around the students' languages would probably improve matters. Further research is needed.

The role of the English teacher

Adopting a plurilingual approach to language teaching requires teachers to change the way they develop activities in class. Using translation proved challenging for this teacher. Despite the English language teacher's constant resort to Catalan or Spanish to explain or to translate unclear concepts, she had never consciously used translation as a tool for learning other languages. This had not been foreseen by the researchers, who had assumed that dealing with a plurilingual setting where plurilingual communication was taking place would be easier than it turned out to be:

> When we were rehearsing today, two pupils said something really weird. Steven was telling me that he was saying his bit in Tagalog but he was actually saying it in English and Sònia said she was saying it in Bengalí when she was really speaking in Catalan. I was really surprised but I imagine that with so many languages they sometimes don't know what they're saying. There are times when I don't really know how to deal with what we are doing.
> (Teacher's diary, April 2009)

At times it seemed that the teacher lacked the skills and confidence required to deal with specific situations like this. The complexities involved in moving towards a plurilingual approach to languages emerged in this context. It cannot be assumed that language teachers have a special sensitivity towards languages and can respond to the misunderstandings and complexities of communicating with pupils with multilevel language competences. It seems that specific training is needed.

To be effective a plurilingual and intercultural approach to language teaching may need to be based on a broad perspective derived from decisions agreed by all the language teachers in a school and adopted as policy by the school as a whole.

Family involvement

Pupils were encouraged to seek help at home, which implied that families would become involved in the project. Too often parents report feeling at a loss because they cannot help their children as they do not speak the language spoken at school. In our study the pupils took the texts home and asked their parents to assess and correct them. The strategies involved in the translation process went beyond the classroom walls as pupils took on the role of interpreter for their families. They found themselves to be 'expert translators', not just passing on the teachers' notes to their families and expecting them to understand the content word-for-word but instead reformulated the information using 'communicative translation' skills suited to their audience.

Our results would suggest that working in a plurilingual manner through the use of translation, in the context of learning a foreign language, is likely to have positive effects on the pupils' language learning and their attitudes towards languages. Assessing whether it is the use of translation per se or the process of valuing pupils' languages through the use of translation requires further research and will be explored in a fuller study.

Conclusion

Promoting plurilingual competence in schools is a necessity in our globalized world. This seems obvious but it is often ignored or considered less important than more traditional academic skills. Coexisting with language diversity does not just entail becoming familiar with other languages and other ways of conceiving the world, but may also give children the plurilingual and intercultural competences they need in both schools and society.

Language learning policies in Europe acknowledge the need for the integration of heritage languages in the classroom (CEFRL, 2001; CCPE, 2009) as part of the goal of promoting plurilingual and intercultural competences in schools. Many good practices are shared and assessed in these policy documents. But in a bilingual context such as the one outlined in this study, where Catalan is fighting to survive against a majority language, Spanish, the emphasis is on promoting the use of Catalan, based on monolingual paradigms that are often ineffective (Vila, 2005).

This study explored the effects of adopting a plurilingual approach to language learning by translating heritage languages in a foreign language classroom through the use of children's literature. The result of this was that children's language proficiency improved in all three school languages, motivation and positive attitudes increased, and there was a little development of pupils' intercultural communicative competence. This fits with research by Cho (2000) and Cummins (2005) on using heritage languages in languages classrooms.

Translation has proved to be a useful learning and teaching tool. Adopting a TOLC approach to translation, and focusing on the acquisition of plurilingual and intercultural skills rather than the language skills per se, was effective in the context we have described here. Instead of being told 'don't translate, try and think in English' pupils were encouraged to translate and to use languages meaningfully in a context that was familiar to them.

Working with children's literature involves not only the linguistic repertoire of the class but also the cultural background of each child. Literature is plural (Hélot, 2011), it is global and it is shared among cultures. It seems, therefore, the ideal starting point in a diverse and plural setting such as this one. The stories created by children remain alive in schools and public libraries, and can be read and referred to year after year.

A similar project designed on a much larger scale could be used to demonstrate how languages can defy the boundaries of homes and schools and different cultures, and become meaningful, visible and useful for pupils of all ages, thus contributing towards the development of an intercultural and plurilingual society.

References

Alcón, E. (2007) 'Linguistic unity and cultural diversity in Europe: Implications for research on English language and learning'. In Alacón, E. and Safont, M. (eds) *Intercultural Language Use and Language Learning*. Dordrecht: Springer, 22–39.

Aronin, L. and Singleton, D. (2012) *Multilingualism*. Amsterdam: John Benjamins Publishing.

Baker, C. (2011) *Foundations of Bilingual Education and Bilingualism*. Clevedon: Multilingual Matters.

Baños, R. (2003) 'Es pot avaluar la competènciadels adolsecents en la comunicació intercultural?' *Temps d'Educació*, 27, 53–71.

Bernaus, M. and Gardner, R.C. (2008) 'Teacher motivation strategies, student perceptions, student motivation, and English achievement'. *The Modern Language Journal*, 92 (3), 387–401.

Bialystok, E. (2001) *Bilingualism in Development: Language, literacy and cognition*. New York: Cambridge University Press.

Carle, E. (1969) *The Very Hungry Caterpillar*. New York: World Publishing Company.

CCPE (Currículum de Primària, Departament d'Educació, Generalitat de Catalunya) (2009) Online. www.xtec.cat/web/curriculum/primaria/curriculum (accessed 10 June 2014).

CEFRL (Common European Framework for Languages) (2001) Online. www.coe.int/t/dg4/education/elp/elp-reg/Source/Key_reference/CEFR_EN.pdf (accessed 16 June 2014).

Cenoz, J. and Genesee, G. (1998) *Beyond Bilingualism: Multilingualism and multilingual education*. Clevedon: Multilingual Matters.

Cenoz, J. and Valencia, J.F. (1994) 'Additive trilingualism: Evidence from the Basque Country'. *Applied Psycholinguistics*, 15 (2), 195–207.

Cho, G. (2000) 'The role of heritage language in social interactions and relationships: Reflections from a language minority group'. *Bilingual Research Journal*, 24 (4), 333–48.

Clyne, M. (2003) 'Towards a more language-centered approach to plurilingualism'. In Dewaele, J.M., Housen, A. and Wei, L. (eds) *Bilingualism: Beyond basic principles*. Clevedon: Multilingual Matters, 43–55.

Cook, G. (2010) *Translation in Language Teaching*. Oxford: Oxford University Press.

Cook, V. (2001) 'Using the first language in the classroom'. *Canadian Modern Language Review*, 57 (3), 184–206.

— (2003) 'Introduction: The changing L1 in the L2 user's mind'. In Cook, V. (ed.) *Effects of the Second Language on the First*. Clevedon: Multilingual Matters, 1–18.

— (2007) 'Multi-competence: Black hole or worm hole for second language acquisition research?' In Zhaonhong, H. (ed.) *Understanding Second Language Process*. Clevedon: Multilingual Matters, 16–26.

Corcoll, C. (2012) 'Developing plurilingual competences with young learners: We play and we learn and we speak in three languages'. In González Davies, M. and Taronna, A. (eds) *New Trends in Early Foreign Language Learning: The Age Factor, CLIL and Languages in Contact: Bridging research and good practices*. Newcastle: Cambridge Scholars Publishing, 16–26.

Cummins, J. (1979) 'Cognitive/academic language proficiency, linguistic interdependence, the optimum age question and some other matters'. *Working Papers on Bilingualism*, 19, 121–9.

— (1984) *Bilingualism and Special Education: Issues in assessment and pedagogy*. Clevedon: Multilingual Matters.

— (2005) 'A proposal for action: Strategies for recognizing heritage language competence as a learning resource within the mainstream classroom'. *The Modern Language Journal*, 89 (4), 585–92.

— (2007) 'Rethinking monolingual instruction in multilingual classrooms'. *Canadian Journal of Applied Linguistics*, 10 (2), 221–40.

Escobar, C. and Unamuno, V. (2008) 'Languages and language learning in Catalan schools: From the bilingual to the multilingual challenge'. In Hélot, C. and de Mejía, A.-M. (eds) *Forging Multilingual Spaces: Integrated perspectives on majority and minority bilingual education*. Bristol: Multilingual Matters, 228–55.

Espainouvingut (2013) Online. www.xtec.cat/web/projectes/alumnatnou (accessed 31 August 2013).

Goitia, V. and Sugranyes, C. (2011) 'The foreign language classroom: A positive context for promoting plurilingualism'. *Apac of News 2011*, 73, 24–30.

González Davies, M. (2011) 'Engaging future generations in multicultural projects through the translation of literature for young readers'. In Clermont, P. and Benert, B. (eds) *Contre l'innocence: Esthétique de l'engagement en littérature de jeunesse*. Frankfurt: Peter Lang, 439–51.

— (2012) 'The comeback of translation: Integrating a spontaneous practice in foreign language learning'. In González Davies, M. and Taronna, A. (eds) *Early Foreign Language Learning in Educational Contexts: Bridging good practices and research*. Newcastle: Cambridge Scholars Publishing, 86–97.

— (forthcoming) 'Towards a plurilingual development paradigm, from spontaneous to informed use of translation in additional language learning'. *Special Issue of The Interpreter and Translator Trainer*, 8 (1).

Guasch, O. (2010) 'El tractament integrat de les àrees de lengua'. In Guasch, O. (ed.) *El tractament integrat de les llengües*. Barcelona: Graó, 7–12.

Hélot, C. (2011) 'Children's literature in the multilingual classroom'. In Hélot, C. and O'Laoire, M. (eds) *Language Policy for the Multilingual Classroom: Pedagogy of the possible*. Clevedon: Multilingual Matters, 42–64.

Hélot, C. and O'Laoire, M. (2011) 'Introduction: From language education policies to a pedagogy of the possible'. In Hélot, C. and O'Laoire, M. (eds) *Language Policy for the Multilingual Classroom: Pedagogy of the possible*. Clevedon: Multilingual Matters, ix–xxii.

Herdina, P. and Jessner, U. (2002) *Perspectives of Change in Psycholinguistics*. Clevedon: Multilingual Matters.

Hervey, S., Higgins, I. and Haywood, L. (1995) *Thinking Spanish Translation*. London, New York: Routledge.

Hill, E. (1983) *Where's Spot?* London: Penguin.

IDESCAT (Institut d'Estadístca de Catalunya) (2013) Online. www.idescat.com (accessed 2 September 2013).

Lasagabaster, D. (1997) '*Creatividad y conciencia metalingüística: Incidencia en el aprendizaje del Inglés como L3*'. Leioa: University of the Basque Country.

Leonardi, V. (2012) 'I know you are Italian, but please think in English! The role of L1 in the EFL classes'. In González Davies, M. and Taronna, A. (eds) *Early Foreign Language Learning in Educational Contexts: Bridging good practices and research*. Newcastle: Cambridge Scholars Publishing, 110–20.

Martin, B. (2007) *Brown Bear, Brown Bear, What do you See?* London: Penguin.

Richards, J. and Rodgers, T. (2001) *Approaches and Methods in Language Teaching*. Cambridge: Cambridge University Press.

Serra Bonet, J.M. (2010) 'Escola, llengua i immigració a Catalunya, algunes reflexions'. *Llengua Societat i Communicació LSC*, 8, 27–34.

Vila, I. (2005) 'Cohesió social i llengua Catalana: Raons per fer del Català la Llengua Vehicular del Sistema Educatiu de Catalunya'. Paper presented at the Segones Jornades del Grup Catalàde Sociolingüística i del Centre Universitari de Sociolingüística Llengua i Ensenyament, Barcelona, November.

Part Two

New pedagogies of multiliteracy

Metalinguistic awareness, multimodality and funds of knowledge

Chapter 4

Children's literature as a catalyst for dual language awareness
Roy Lyster

Introduction
This chapter is about collaboration between partner teachers (teachers of French and English to the same students) who used children's literature to enhance their students' morphological awareness across languages. The teachers co-designed and implemented biliteracy tasks associated with the French and English editions of illustrated storybooks that they read aloud in their classes. I report how the storybooks were employed to highlight cross-lingual connections between languages and discuss the effects of the biliteracy instruction on students' awareness of derivational morphology. Also, I highlight innovative ways to make use of children's literature as a rich source of content that stimulates student motivation and language growth.

Biliteracy instruction
Biliteracy instruction, which targets two languages rather than only one, is backed by research advocating cross-lingual connections that intentionally activate the first language (L1) as a cognitive resource to support second language (L2) learning (e.g. Cook, 2001; Swain and Lapkin, 2013). Cummins has led with his argument that 'learning efficiencies can be achieved if teachers explicitly draw students' attention to similarities and differences between their languages and reinforce effective learning strategies in a coordinated way across languages' (2007: 233). Cummins has identified a common underlying proficiency that allows skills and concepts learned through one language to be transferred to another (Cummins, 2000). He argues that, because cross-lingual transfer is occurring as a normal process of bilingual development, 'it seems reasonable to teach for two-way cross-lingual transfer (L1 to L2, L2 to L1) in order to render the process as effective as possible' (Cummins, 2007: 231).

Cross-lingual instructional strategies serve to subvert what Cummins calls 'the two solitudes assumption' (2007: 229), by which target languages are kept separate, so that time allotted for one language is restricted to the exclusive use of that language, typically with no reference to the other, even though literacy in both languages (biliteracy) is the goal. Soltero-González *et al.* similarly advocate a 'holistic bilingual perspective' of biliteracy development, specifically with respect to writing abilities, whereby 'knowledge and literacy competencies in both languages support development for one another' (2012: 72). In the same vein, Cenoz and Gorter advocate a 'focus on multilingualism approach' that 'highlights the relationships between languages by creating specific activities so as to enhance metalinguistic awareness' (2011: 360).

But how can teachers effectively encourage emergent bilinguals to draw on their knowledge of both languages while developing a sense of linguistic and contextual integrity for each language on its own? Language teachers want answers to this question because competition between target languages for time and status in school settings often leads to the habitual use of one language over the other, so the notion of each language having its own space becomes crucial.

The present study was designed to address this issue by focusing on collaboration between partner teachers who teach different languages to the same group of students. The partner teachers co-designed and implemented biliteracy tasks that began in one language during its allotted class time and continued in the other language during its class time. In this way, each target language remained the language of communication in its respective classroom, even though borders between languages and classrooms were crossed as students engaged with the themes of the storybooks in both languages and engaged in activities highlighting derivational patterns specific to each language and common to both.

Morphological awareness

The overall target of the intervention in this study is morphological awareness, defined by Carlisle as the 'conscious awareness of the morphemic structure of words and ability to reflect on and manipulate that structure' (1995: 194). Morphological awareness encompasses three types of morphology (Kuo and Anderson, 2006): (1) inflections (e.g. morphemes added to verbs to mark person or tense and to nouns to mark number); (2) derivatives (e.g. morphemes added to a base morpheme to change its meaning or syntactic category); and (3) compounds (i.e. combinations of two or more words or roots).

The specific target of the present study was derivational morphology, which research had identified as problematic for Canadian French immersion students whose lexical proficiency was found to lack richness compared with that of native speakers of the same age, specifically with respect to derivational morphology. Harley and King (1989) reported that immersion students underused derived verbs such as *affoler* and *encercler*, and Harley (1992) noted their underuse of derivational prefixes. For example, to express the notion of going back to sleep, they avoided using the prefix *re-* in derived verbs such *se rendormir* and *se recoucher*, and opted instead for the root form of the verb followed by the adverb *encore* (i.e. 'again') as in *dormir encore* or *coucher encore*.

Immersion students' limited use of derivation in their L2 production was explained in the light of research that revealed considerable emphasis in immersion classrooms on learning the meaning of difficult words at the expense of attention to the structural and generative properties of words (Allen *et al.*, 1990). For years researchers have consequently recommended explicit vocabulary instruction in immersion settings that includes cross-lingual teaching strategies and reference to cognates, to alert students to differences and similarities between their L1 and L2 (Allen *et al.*, 1990; Clipperton, 1994; Harley and King, 1989). One way to do so is through morphological instruction, defined as 'instruction about any element of oral or written morphology (including prefixes, suffixes, bases or roots, compounds, derivations, and inflections)' (Bowers *et al.*, 2010: 150).

There is convincing evidence that morphological instruction: (1) improves reading comprehension (e.g. Carlisle, 2000; Kuo and Anderson, 2006); (2) increases 'motivation to investigate words' (Bowers *et al.*, 2010: 145); and (3) develops vocabulary well beyond the words targeted by the instruction (Bowers and Kirby, 2010). Bowers *et al.*'s (2010) meta-analysis of 22 studies of morphological instruction from pre-kindergarten (age 4) to Grade 8 (age 14) revealed positive effects, especially for younger learners when the intervention was combined with other aspects of literacy instruction. Inspired by this meta-analysis, the present study drew on its results by implementing morphological instruction with 7- to 8-year-old children in the context of biliteracy units co-designed by their French and English teachers and based on the themes of illustrated storybooks.

Context and background

Canada is an officially bilingual country (French/English), with about 22 per cent of its 34 million inhabitants claiming French as their home language and 67 per cent English. The majority of French speakers are concentrated in the province of Quebec, where 80 per cent of its 8 million inhabitants claim French as their home language and only 8 per cent claim English. The largest urban setting in Quebec is the city of Greater Montreal, where 69 per cent of its 3.8 million inhabitants claim French as their home language and 13 per cent claim English. Within this context, where the study took place, there are two distinct school systems: one designated as French-speaking and the other as English-speaking. French immersion programmes, in which at least 50 per cent of the curriculum is taught in French, are found in schools designated as English-speaking. There are no equivalent English immersion programmes in French-speaking schools, where all subject matter is required by law to be taught exclusively in French.

The school board in which this study unfolded serves about ten thousand students across a large territory along the South Shore of Montreal and is officially designated as English-speaking. This designation allows it to provide schooling to students holding a certificate of eligibility for English education in Quebec: that is, students with at least one parent (or sibling) having attended an English school in Canada. All other children are required by law to attend schools designated as French-speaking. Although officially designated as an English-speaking school board, 38 per cent of its elementary students in 2005 claimed French as their home language, only 53 per cent claimed English, and 9 per cent claimed another language (Hobbs and Nasso-Maselli, 2005). The high number of French-speaking children in an English-speaking school board is the result of cases where, even though French might be claimed as the home language, one parent (or sibling) had attended an English speaking school in Canada and so the parents exercise their right to send their children to an English-speaking school. Their intention is to foster a degree of French-English bilingualism in their children that would be difficult to attain in French-speaking schools.

The study reported here built on a previous study undertaken by myself and colleagues (Lyster *et al.*, 2009) in partnership with the same school board. In collaboration with six teachers, we implemented a Bilingual Read-Aloud Project whereby the French and English teachers of each class read aloud to their students (ranging in age from 6 to 8) from the same three chapter books over four months, alternating the reading of one chapter in the French class with another in the English class. Written by Mary Pope Osborne, the books were part of the Magic Tree House series, published in English by Random House and in French as the Cabane Magique series by Bayard Jeunesse.

Students participated enthusiastically during the reading of the stories in the two languages. This appeared to enable the students to understand the stories, whatever their language dominance. Moreover, their interest in going on to read stories on their own from the same book series was striking. During the read-aloud sessions, propitious opportunities arose for students to learn a new concept along with new words in both languages, yet there was little systematic collaboration among teachers to make connections across languages. The researchers concluded that to exploit the potential of such a project for facilitating teacher collaboration on language-based objectives to the full would require more time for participating teachers to actually collaborate on planning, as well as more structured guidance regarding the language focus.

This conclusion provided the impetus for a two-year professional development project, called Teacher Collaboration for Integrated Language Learning (TCILL), which is the focus of the present chapter. The project was funded by the Québec Ministère de l'Éducation, du Loisir et du Sport (MELS), which enabled participating teachers to be released from their teaching duties so that they could take part in a series of professional development workshops. Year 1 served as a pilot study, while Year 2 developed into a quasi-experimental study embedded in the professional development project.

The goals of the two-year professional development initiative were firstly to create curricular coherence across French and English classes, secondly to facilitate collaboration between French and English teachers, and thirdly to strengthen students' vocabulary knowledge in both languages. These goals were in line with the school board's commitment to implementing Professional Learning Communities (DuFour *et al.*, 2008), which involve collaborative efforts to assess evidence of student success and to make adjustments accordingly to ensure the delivery of high-quality instructional activities. Given the board's commitment to team efforts for improving instructional practice, along with the new blend of L1 and L2 learners in the same classrooms, the time was ripe for a professional development initiative designed to facilitate collaboration between the teachers of English and French.

Pilot study

Year 1 allowed us to pilot various approaches to the professional development component of the TCILL project. In six half-day sessions over the school year at the school board office, seven teachers of Grades 1 and 2 worked with the English and French language consultants from the school board. The professional development sessions included workshops on vocabulary instruction and the use of storybooks as language teaching resources. Other sessions were devoted to creating biliteracy tasks to be implemented in the context of various illustrated storybooks, such as the French and English versions of *Catch That Cat!* (Poulin, 2003), *When Stella Was Very, Very Small* (Gay, 2009), *That's Hockey* (Bouchard, 2002), *The Balloon Tree* (Gilman, 2004) and *The Three Robbers* (Ungerer, 2008).

The following example is a prototypical biliteracy task that emerged from these collaborative efforts in Year 1 and whose procedures were adopted during Year 2. The teacher of one language read aloud *The Three Robbers* (in French, *Les trois brigands*), but stopped when she reached an important point in the story, when the protagonist discovered the robbers' hidden treasures and asked them how they would spend all their money. The teacher asked students to make oral predictions about how they thought the money might be spent and then to illustrate their predictions along with written annotations. In the next class, in the other language, the teacher asked students to retell their predictions and then read the rest of the story, and compared the students' predictions with the written ending: 'They set off and gathered up all the lost, unhappy, and abandoned children they could find ... and they bought a beautiful castle where all of them could live.'

The students' attention was then drawn to derivational morphology – by the English teacher who pointed out the use and meaning of the prefix *un-* in *unhappy* and by the French teacher who pointed out the use and meaning of the prefix *mal-* in *malheureux*. The teachers followed up in their respective classes with tasks or games requiring other words to be formed by analogy with the same prefixes. In English, this included adjectives such as *unable* and *unbelievable* and verbs such as *unfold* and *unpack*. In one class, the teacher covertly asked individual students to mime words such as *unfold* or *unpack* for the others to guess what action was being mimed. In French, teachers drew attention to adjectives such as *malhonnête* and *malpoli* but because *mal-* is limited in its use as an adjectival prefix, they extended their focus to include the much more productive prefix *in-* in words such as *incapable* and *incroyable*.

Main study

Year 2 of the TCILL project entailed a similar set of professional development workshops and also a set of pre- and post-intervention measures designed to assess the effects of the biliteracy instruction over time. In addition to measuring the overall effects of biliteracy instruction on morphological awareness in both French and English, the study was designed to explore what type of learner (English-dominant, French-dominant, bilingual) in what type of programme (English-dominant, French-dominant, bilingual) improves most in morphological awareness in each language.

Participants

Year 2 of the TCILL project began with a cohort of ten teachers (eight women and two men), all with previous teaching experience, in addition to three lead teachers (all women) who, having participated in Year 1, agreed to play a mentoring role during Year 2. Other participants in the professional development activities during Year 2 included three researchers from the university and the English and French language consultants (also women) from the school board. Of the teachers who participated throughout all of Year 2, only one had training in L2 education (i.e. a certificate in teaching French L2) and one other had completed a BA in Psychology and Linguistics prior to undertaking her BEd in elementary education. All the rest had training in elementary education with no specialization in either L2 teaching or linguistics.

Among the cohort of ten teachers, the two men shared two classes in a 50/50 French/English bilingual programme: a Grade 2 class (n=23) and a Grade 2/3 class (n=18). A second pair of teachers taught a Grade 2 class (n=22) in a French immersion programme with 80 per cent of its curriculum in French and 20 per cent in English. A third pair taught a Grade 2 class (n=17) in an English stream programme with 80 per cent of its curriculum in English and 20 per cent in French. A fourth pair taught a Grade 2/3 class (n=18) also in an English stream programme (80 per cent English + 20 per cent French). The French teacher of this class had to withdraw from the project due to ill health, but the English teacher continued, collaborating with other participating teachers from her school. The fifth pair taught a Grade 1 class (n=16) in a French immersion programme (80 per cent French + 20 per cent English).

Participating teachers thus represented three different programmes with different proportions of instructional time in the target languages: (1) 80 per cent French + 20 per cent English; (2) 50 per cent French + 50 per cent English; and (3) 20 per cent French + 80 per cent English. Although our initial intention was to work with the French and English teachers of French immersion students (in programmes ranging from 50 per cent to 80 per cent in French), the school board was keen on opening the project up to non-immersion programmes as well. This allowed us to investigate the extent to which varying the proportions of target languages across the curriculum might influence biliteracy instruction and its effects on student outcomes.

To measure the effects of biliteracy instruction on student outcomes, a Morphological Awareness Test (described below) was administered to a subsample of 45 students (23 girls, 22 boys) exposed to the biliteracy instruction (i.e. the experimental group) and to a comparison group of 20 students (7 girls, 13 boys) from two schools in the same school board whose teachers were not participants in the TCILL project. Convenience sampling was used to recruit students for testing, with those who had returned signed parental consent forms being selected (n=78). Of the 58 students in the experimental group, three were in Grade 3 so their data were not used in the final analyses; the five from the class whose French teacher was unable to implement the treatment were excluded and five others were excluded from the analyses because they did not complete all the tests. In total, therefore, results from 45 experimental students and 20 comparison students were analysed.

The Peabody Picture Vocabulary Test – Fourth Edition (PPVT-4; Dunn and Dunn, 2007) and its French equivalent, *Échelle de vocabulaire en images Peabody* (EVIP; Dunn *et al.*, 1993) were used as standardized measures of receptive vocabulary for identifying individual students' dominant language because previous experience in our programme of research suggested that reports of a child's home language – whether provided by the child, teacher or parent – were unreliable indicators of the child's actual language dominance. We used raw scores to calculate the difference for each individual between the English and French versions and then a percentage of how many more words were identified in one language than the other. What then proved most effective for forming three groups based on these per cent differentials was to consider participants dominant in one language if they identified a minimum of 20 per cent more words in it than in the other language. Students classified as English-dominant identified an average of 58 per cent more words in English than in French, whereas students classified as French-dominant identified an average of 35 per cent more words in French than in English. Students classified as bilingual identified a similar proportion of words in both languages, with on average only 1 per cent more in one of the languages. The distribution of all 65 student participants according to treatment condition, programme type and language dominance appears in Table 4.1.

Table 4.1: Distribution of participants (experimental + comparison) by programme type and language dominance

	80% French programme	50% French programme	20% French programme	Total
English-dominant students	6 + 2	3 + 0	0 + 6	9 + 8 = 17
French-dominant students	1 + 4	8 + 0	7 + 1	16 + 5 = 21
Bilingual students	7 + 4	10 + 0	3 + 3	20 + 7 = 27
Total	14 + 10 = 24	21 + 0 = 21	10 + 10 = 20	45 + 20 = 65

Professional development workshops

Five day-long workshops were held for all participants at the school board office throughout Year 2. The first (November 2011) began with an overview of the project provided by videos from the Bilingual Read-Aloud Project (Lyster *et al.*, 2009) and videos from Year 1, and then explored the use of illustrated storybooks for teaching language and enhancing biliteracy skills. The second workshop (December 2011) covered two topics: vocabulary instruction and teacher collaboration. Vocabulary instruction was elaborated as a means to focus not only on meaning for comprehension but also on the structural and generative properties of words, while reflection on teacher collaboration was initiated by viewing a video about collaboration between a language arts teacher and a visual arts teacher called *Revealing Character* (Annenberg Foundation, 2012). Teachers were then given the opportunity to test the waters of collaboration as they worked together on designing tasks to accompany *The Three Robbers* (Ungerer, 2008), which they could then opt to use with their students or not. The third and fourth sessions (February and March 2012) were devoted to collaboration between partner teachers who co-designed biliteracy tasks to accompany their reading aloud to students of *Moon Man* (Ungerer, 2009) and *Crictor* (Ungerer, 1958), respectively.

Following each of these sessions, our research team made visits to the schools to videotape the implementation of at least four lessons (two in each language) that the teachers had co-designed for each storybook. The fifth and final professional development session (June 2012) was structured around viewing the videotaped lessons, and this initiated a stimulated-recall procedure that allowed teachers to discuss their mutual implementation of co-designed interventions as well as their students' involvement in both target languages.

Instructional treatments

The instructional treatments drew on the components of a counterbalanced approach that integrates form-focused and content-based instruction in ways that encourage shifts in students' attention between language and content (Lyster, 2007). While the language focus was on derivational morphology, the content focus emerged from the themes of illustrated storybooks.

In the Bilingual Read-Aloud Project the chapters were read alternately in English and French (Lyster *et al.*, 2009). However, the illustrated storybooks used in the present study had no chapters, so some of the partner teachers read the storybooks at least once in each language, while others alternated between languages, reading short sections in each. In contrast to Year 1, which began with a focus on books by Canadian authors (Stéphane Poulin, Caroline Gay, David Bouchard), Year 2 focused on illustrated storybooks by Tomi Ungerer, an award-winning illustrator and multilingual author from Alsace, who was chosen by the Council of Europe as its Ambassador for Childhood and Education in 2003. We learned from both the teachers and students in Year 1 that they greatly appreciated focusing on a single author. So the focus on Tomi Ungerer in Year 2 was welcomed, the more so because few of the participants knew his work and liked being exposed to something new.

The instructional interventions, which lasted roughly 8–10 hours (4–5 hours each for *Moon Man* and *Crictor*), were not expected to be identical in every classroom. The professional development component emphasized collaboration between partner teachers, who were invited to draw on their own creativity to adapt the linguistic resources provided during the workshops to their own teaching styles and the students' needs. Two things remained constant across the intervention: the storybooks and their themes, and the emphasis on derivational morphology as outlined in the materials provided to teachers during the workshops. The teachers received a four-page document in each language for *Moon Man* and a six-page document for *Crictor* suggesting various word-focused tasks. These tasks included the prefixes *dis-* and *un-* in English and *dé-*, *in-* and *mal-* in French. Suffixes in English included *-able, -al, -ible, -ful, -ic, -ity, -ness, -ous, -sion* and *-tion*, while those in French included *-able, -al, -eur, -eux, -ible, -ier, -ique, -iste, -ment, -té* and *-tion*. The focus was thus on bound morphemes and on suffixes more frequently than on prefixes.

An example of a word-focused task suggested to teachers for the English version of *Moon Man* concerned the adjective *mysterious*, which appears as a key word to describe the protagonist. It was suggested that English teachers help students to recognize the noun *mystery* as the base of *mysterious* and to form and identify similarly formed adjectives (e.g. *courageous* from *courage*) or nouns (e.g. *disaster* from *disastrous*). The word *courageux* appears in the French version, so French teachers helped students to identify the noun *courage* as its base and generate similarly constructed adjectives (e.g. *paresseux* from *paresse*) or nouns (e.g. *mystère* from *mystérieux*).

How the instructional interventions were implemented is illustrated through the way the book *Crictor* was used. Crictor is a boa constrictor given as a gift to Mme Bodot, a schoolteacher living in Paris. She goes out of her way to make Crictor feel comfortable in her home, installing a long bed for him alongside palm trees and even knitting him a long scarf. In turn, Crictor makes himself useful at her school, helping the children learn to count, read the alphabet and tie knots, and serving as a slide and a skipping rope. Crictor saves Mme Bodot from a burglar who has gagged her and tied her up, and so becomes a hero, is awarded a medal for his bravery and has a statue erected in his honour.

During the planning sessions, teachers were given a six-page document in each language with suggested word-focused tasks for them to integrate into their co-designed thematic units on *Crictor*, and key vocabulary items for teachers to focus on in English and French (see Figures 4.1 and 4.2). Accordingly, as they read the story aloud to emphasize the theme of heroism and the heroic attributes of Crictor, the English teachers drew attention to key words such as *helpful, faithful, honour* and *respected*, while French teachers highlighted their French equivalents: *serviable, fidèle, honneur* and *respecté*.

One of the English teachers engaged students in a typical follow-up word-focused task: using prefixes (*un-* and *dis-*) to form antonyms (i.e. *unhelpful, unfaithful, dishonour, disrespected*) as they made up alternative endings to the story. The derivational relationships in reference to Crictor's heroic traits were emphasized by the words *hero* and *heroism* in the English class and *héros* and *héroisme* in the French class. English teachers drew attention to the suffix *-ic* in *heroic* to encourage students to discover similar derivations (e.g. *science* → *scientific*; *history* → *historic*), while French teachers drew attention to the suffix *-ique* in *héroïque* to encourage students to discover analogous derivations in French (e.g. *science* → *scientifique*; *histoire* → *historique*). Still other word-focused tasks deemed appropriate and relevant by the teachers dwelt on similar patterns of suffixation in words whose meanings were closely tied to the story (e.g. *courage* → *courageous* or *courageux*; *danger* → *dangerous* or *dangereux*).

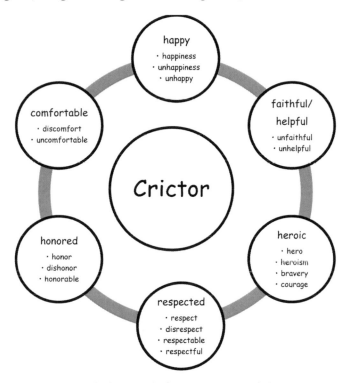

Figure 4.1: Vocabulary guide for *Crictor* in English

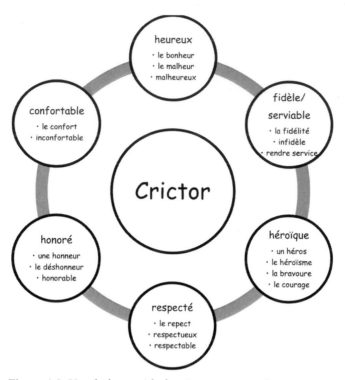

Figure 4.2: Vocabulary guide for *Crictor* in French

In Year 2 a pair of teachers co-designed and implemented a biliteracy task related to *Crictor* on the theme of adaptation, which they thought underpinned the narrative: while Mme Bodot helped Crictor to adapt to his new home, Crictor was adapting to his new community by being so helpful. So the teachers presented students with information about four other animals (giraffes, octopuses, porcupines and bats) to interest them in imagining having one as a pet. After orally brainstorming various scenarios, students in the English class each created an annotated illustration depicting what they would do to help their pet adapt to its new home, while in the French class they made an annotated illustration of how the same pet would adapt to its new community by being helpful. The final product was a bilingual class book portraying each student's contribution in French and English on facing pages.

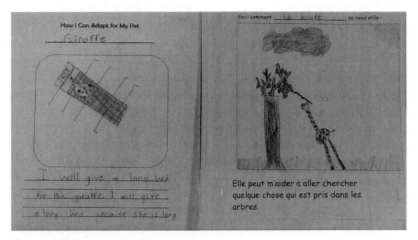

Photograph by Susan Ballinger

Figure 4.3: A student's annotated illustrations appearing in the bilingual class book

Data collection

Two versions of a 40-item Morphological Awareness Test (MAT; Quiroga, 2013) – one in English and the other in French – were developed and validated specifically to serve as the primary measure for assessing the effects of the biliteracy instruction. The students completed the 40 items in 20 to 30 minutes on average, by talking with a researcher orally for each language on different days while looking at the items on a test sheet. Administered as a pre-test in January to February before the instructional treatment and as a post-test afterwards in May to June, both versions included a balance of familiar and unfamiliar items as about half of them had appeared in the word-focused tasks provided to teachers during the workshops. In line with the instruction, more test items involved suffixation than prefixation.

The first set of 20 items assessed morphological awareness through processes of analysis; that is, decomposition, requiring students to separate a derived form into its morphemic constituents. For example, when given the word *usefulness*, students were expected to identify *use* as the main word, and *ful* and *ness* as the two extra parts. The second set of 20 items assessed morphological awareness through processes of synthesis; that is, derivation, requiring students to employ knowledge of suffixation to produce a derived form from its base. For example, students heard and saw the sentence, 'If you live in PEACE, you are very _____' and were expected to produce the derived word *peaceful*. The maximum number of points a student could achieve on the MAT was 146. Details of the scoring as well as the validation procedures and reliability statistics can be found in Lyster *et al.* (2013).

In addition to the testing, participating teachers were interviewed in their pairs in December and again in June. The first interview served to ascertain their linguistic and educational backgrounds, their previous collaboration experiences with colleagues, their approach to vocabulary instruction and their reasons for participating in the project. The second interview served to capture their impressions of the collaborative process and the professional development component of the project, the storybooks used, and their students' reactions to the biliteracy intervention. At the same time, in June, teachers were asked to complete a questionnaire, also eliciting their impressions of the feasibility of collaboration with their colleague and their perceptions of its effects on their students.

Finally the instructional treatments were videotaped where possible, yielding approximately 12.5 hours of video-recorded lessons across four pairs of teachers and their five intact classes. Scheduling more class visits for videotaping proved challenging for the research team because most of the lessons were held at roughly the same time, so to provide a more complete portrait of the instructional treatments, teachers submitted lesson plans. At the final day-long meeting in June, they shared with colleagues artefacts that had been created for use during their interventions or produced by the students as a result.

Results
Learning outcomes
The details of the quantitative analyses appear in Lyster *et al.* (2013), so only a brief synopsis is presented here. The experimental group significantly outperformed the comparison group in French at post-testing, but not in English. The positive effects in French were similar for all students receiving the instruction irrespective of language dominance or programme type. Although students receiving the instruction did not, as a group, outperform students not receiving the instruction in English, the analysis of the MAT scores revealed a significant difference between English-dominant students receiving the instruction and those who did not.

That the effects of the instructional treatment were more robust in French than in English remains open to interpretation. It may be due to the delivery of the instruction in French, where there is greater emphasis on metalinguistic awareness and structural analysis. Instruction in English places more emphasis on language development through whole language approaches that take precedence over language analysis. The French teachers with training in mother tongue education may have focused on language analysis more than the English teachers with training in English language arts did, thus priming the students for a stronger metalinguistic focus. This is purely speculative and was not an issue during the workshops or in the qualitative data. If there was such a disparity between partner teachers, it can be said to have contributed to a positive synergy and complementarity during the collaborative process.

Teacher collaboration

The research team benefited from having piloted the professional development component of the project during Year 1, because three of the teachers from Year 1 became lead teachers during Year 2, guiding their colleagues in task design and giving them moral support. Thanks to them, the six half-day professional development Year 1 sessions were extended to five full-day sessions during Year 2. The longer sessions plus the lead teachers' mentoring greatly enhanced the collaborative process in Year 2. It was apparent that 'institutional commitments to provide teachers with sufficient time and sustainable opportunities for peer coaching in the spirit of cross-disciplinary collaboration' enabled teachers to maximize their professional development (Lyster and Ballinger, 2011: 286).

The teachers were enthusiastic about the project. They especially appreciated the time to collaborate and were impressed by their students' positive reactions to the biliteracy instruction, saying that students 'loved it' and 'enjoyed making connections between the two languages'. Even before the test results were known, they were convinced that the biliteracy instruction focusing on derivational morphology had been effective. As one teacher put it, her students were commenting on word formation during other activities: 'They would say, "Oh look! A little word inside a big word!"'

We had been concerned that using the same storybook in each language would bore the children or create confusion rather than coherence, but the teachers were unanimous that the pupils were neither bored nor confused. As one teacher stated, 'The kids responded well to the lessons, and they saw that they were intertwined, and they liked the reading of the English book and the French book.' They unanimously ranked *Crictor* as their favourite book, followed by *Moon Man*. One pair of teachers integrated *Crictor* with their theme of reptiles and *Moon Man* with their theme of space, focusing on planets in English class and the moon in French class. Teachers found *The Three Robbers* harder to integrate thematically and one pair qualified it as 'kind of dark for little kids' and were pleased that it had been optional to use it.

All the teachers appreciated the professional development component and how the TCILL workshops had such a good balance of theory and hands-on activities. All teachers commented on the merits of having time to collaborate and to benefit, at the same time, from guidance provided by both colleagues and researchers to support their collaboration. One teacher extolled the benefits of having lead teachers acting as mentors: 'They knew where to go, they knew how it worked, and they helped a lot.' Some partner teachers had already been collaborating before the projects, most notably the French teacher and English teacher in the 50/50 programme. Others were new to cross-lingual collaboration, and said that, at their schools, collaboration more typically involved teachers within content areas at the same grade level rather than across languages. One of the English teachers remarked that her previous attempts at collaboration had involved 'more superficial collaboration, like for example, "Oh, I hear you're doing bugs in your class. OK, I'll do some bug stuff too".' Whereas much of the research on teacher collaboration in language education has focused on collaboration between content and language specialists (e.g. Arkoudis, 2006; Creese, 2002; Creese, 2006; Short, 2002), the present study has added a new perspective with its focus on collaboration specifically between teachers of different target languages.

Students' age and motivation

It was initially thought that older children might be better suited to a focus on derivational morphology, in accordance with Kuo and Anderson's (2006) observation that children usually begin to develop explicit awareness of the structure and meaning of derived forms at around Grades 3 or 4. Our decision to target students at Grade 2 level was a response to the school board's request for the research team to work with teachers at that level because teachers of higher grades were already engaged in other professional development activities. This created an opportunity for us to assess the feasibility and effectiveness of biliteracy instruction of younger learners just beginning to develop literacy. In line with previous research (e.g. Bowers *et al.*, 2010; Kuo and Anderson, 2006), our study indicates the feasibility and benefits of a much earlier start. As Bowers *et al.* (2010: 148) observe, 'If morphological instruction were introduced early in literacy learning, morphological knowledge would have time to become consolidated and have more opportunities to contribute to literacy learning'.

An especially positive result of the present study was the enthusiasm exhibited by the children during the instructional interventions, as reported by their teachers, and captured on the video. In the same vein, Bowers *et al.* (2010: 171) reported that several of the authors of the studies included in their meta-analysis 'commented on the enthusiasm children showed during morphological instruction'. While acknowledging that measures of motivation were not actually used, Bowers and colleagues suggested that 'increased motivation and literacy skills may mutually support each other'. We believe that the enthusiasm of the young children in our study as they adopted a detective-like approach to morphological derivation contributed to their significant improvement. This fits with Lambert and Tucker's (1972: 208) seminal research on French immersion programmes in which they found very young students to have a 'children's version of contrastive linguistics' and a linguistic 'detective' capacity: 'an attentive, patient, inductive concern with words, meanings, and linguistic regularities'.

Conclusion

The between-group comparisons in our study revealed the improvement in French by the group exposed to the instruction, whatever the language dominance or programme type. In the case of English, only students identified as English-dominant scored significantly higher in the experimental group than their counterparts in the comparison group. This supports previous research demonstrating that the development of morphological awareness and its crossover effects are language-specific (Deacon *et al.*, 2007; Kuo and Anderson, 2006; Pasquarella *et al.*, 2011).

Further investigation is warranted to explore the reasons for the language-specific outcomes of biliteracy instruction focusing specifically on derivational morphology in French and English. For their part the teachers were enthusiastic about their participation in a professional development initiative that gave them opportunities to co-design tasks based on children's literature to target derivational morphology.

The study described brought together complementary areas of the educational literature advocating an instructional focus on morphological awareness for literacy development and cross-lingual connections for biliteracy development. To target these instructional goals, the TCILL project drew on the dynamics of a partnership between a university and a local school board to engage teachers in a professional development initiative that included peer coaching and collaborative planning. By demonstrating the benefits of collaborative efforts to integrate cross-lingual pedagogy with biliteracy instruction, the project brought children's literature to the fore as a rich and engaging source of language and content for young learners with varying degrees of language proficiency, and from immersion and non-immersion programmes alike.

References

Allen, P., Swain, M., Harley, B. and Cummins J. (1990) 'Aspects of classroom treatment: Toward a more comprehensive view of second language education'. In Harley, B., Allen, P., Cummins, J. and Swain. M. (eds) *The Development of Second Language Proficiency*. Cambridge: Cambridge University Press, 57–81.

Annenberg Foundation (Producer) (2012) *Revealing Character*. Online. www.learner.org/libraries/connectarts68/01_revealing/01program_video. html?pop=yes?pop=yes&pid=2132# (accessed 5 June 2014).

Arkoudis, S. (2006) 'Negotiating the rough ground between ESL and mainstream teachers'. *International Journal of Bilingual Education and Bilingualism*, 9 (4), 415–33.

Bouchard, D. (2002) *That's Hockey*. Victoria, BC: Orca Books.

Bowers, P.N. and Kirby, J.R. (2010) 'Effects of morphological instruction on vocabulary acquisition'. *Reading and Writing: An Interdisciplinary Journal*, 23, 515–37.

Bowers, P.N., Kirby, J.R. and Deacon, H. (2010) 'The effects of morphological instruction on literacy skills: A systematic review of the literature'. *Review of Educational Research*, 80 (2), 144–79.

Carlisle, J. (1995) 'Morphological awareness and early reading achievement'. In Feldman, L.B. (ed.) *Morphological Aspects of Language Processing*. Hillsdale, NJ: Erlbaum, 189–209.

— (2000) 'Awareness of the structure and meaning of morphologically complex words: Impact on reading'. *Reading and Writing: An Interdisciplinary Journal*, 12 (3), 169–90.

Cenoz, J. and Gorter, D. (2011) 'Focus on multilingualism: A study of trilingual writing'. *The Modern Language Journal*, 95 (3), 356–69.

Clipperton, R. (1994) 'Explicit vocabulary instruction in French immersion'. *The Canadian Modern Language Review*, 50, 737–49.

Cook, V. (2001) 'Using the first language in the classroom'. *The Canadian Modern Language Review*, 57, 402–23.

Creese, A. (2002) 'The discursive construction of power in teacher partnerships: Language and subject specialists in mainstream schools'. *TESOL Quarterly*, 36 (4), 597–616.

— (2006) 'Supporting talk? Partnership teachers in classroom interaction'. *International Journal of Bilingual Education and Bilingualism*, 9 (4), 434–53.

Cummins, J. (2000) *Language, Power, and Pedagogy: Bilingual children in the crossfire*. Clevedon: Multilingual Matters.

— (2007) 'Rethinking monolingual instructional strategies in multilingual classrooms'. *Canadian Journal of Applied Linguistics*, 10 (2), 221–41.

Deacon, H., Wade-Woolley, L. and Kirby, J. (2007) 'Crossover: The role of morphological awareness in French immersion children's reading'. *Developmental Psychology*, 3, 732–46.

DuFour, R., DuFour, R.B. and Eaker, R. (2008) *Revisiting Professional Learning Communities at Work: New insights for improving schools*. Bloomington, IN: Solution Tree.

Dunn, L. and Dunn, D. (2007) *Peabody Picture Vocabulary Test, Fourth Edition (PPVT™-4)*. San Antonio, TX: Pearson Education.

Dunn, L., Dunn, L. and Thériault-Whalen, C. (1993) *Échelle de vocabulaire en images Peabody*. Toronto, ON: Pearson Canada Assessment.

Gay, M.-L. (2009) *When Stella Was Very, Very Small*. Toronto, ON: Groundwood Books.

Gilman, P. (2004) *The Balloon Tree*. Originally 1984. Markham, ON: Scholastic Canada.

Harley, B. (1992) 'Patterns of second language development in French immersion'. *Journal of French Language Studies*, 2 (2), 159–83.

Harley, B. and King, M. (1989) 'Verb lexis in the written compositions of young L2 learners'. *Studies in Second Language Acquisition*, 11 (4), 415–39.

Hobbs, J. and Nasso-Maselli, M. (2005) *Elementary Programs Study*. St Lambert, QC: Riverside School Board.

Kuo, L.-J. and Anderson, R.C. (2006) 'Morphological awareness and learning to read: A cross-language perspective'. *Educational Psychologist*, 41 (3), 161–80.

Lambert, W. and Tucker, R. (1972) *Bilingual Education of Children: The St. Lambert experiment*. Rowley, MA: Newbury House.

Lyster, R. (2007) *Learning and Teaching Languages Through Content: A counterbalanced approach*. Amsterdam: John Benjamins.

Lyster, R. and Ballinger, S. (2011) 'Content-based language teaching: Convergent concerns across divergent contexts'. *Language Teaching Research*, 15 (3), 279–88.

Lyster, R., Collins, L. and Ballinger, S. (2009) 'Linking languages through a bilingual read-aloud project'. *Language Awareness*, 18 (3–4), 366–83.

Lyster, R., Quiroga, J. and Ballinger, S. (2013) 'The effects of biliteracy instruction on morphological awareness'. *Journal of Immersion and Content-Based Language Education*, 1 (2), 169–97.

Pasquarella, A., Chen, X., Lam, K. and Luo, Y. (2011) 'Cross-language transfer of morphological awareness in Chinese–English bilinguals'. *Journal of Research in Reading*, 34 (1), 23–42.

Poulin, S. (2003) *Catch That Cat!* Plattsburgh, NY: Tundra Books.

Quiroga, J. (2013) 'Measuring Morphological Awareness Across Languages'. MA thesis, McGill University, Montreal.

Short, D. (2002) 'Language learning in sheltered social studies classes'. *TESOL Journal*, 11, 18–24.

Soltero-González, L., Escamilla, K. and Hopewell, S. (2012) 'Changing teachers' perceptions about the writing abilities of emerging bilingual students: Towards a holistic bilingual perspective on writing assessment'. *International Journal of Bilingual Education and Bilingualism*, 15 (1), 71–94.

Swain, M. and Lapkin, S. (2013) 'A Vygotskian sociocultural perspective on immersion education: The L1/L2 debate'. *Journal of Immersion and Content-Based Education*, 1 (1), 101–29.

Ungerer, T. (1958) *Crictor*. New York: Harper Collins.

— (2008) *The Three Robbers*. Originally 1962. New York: Phaidon.

— (2009) *Moon Man*. Originally 1967. New York: Phaidon.

Chapter 5
DIY plurilingual literature
A multimodal approach to linguistic inclusion in the urban elementary classroom

Heather Lotherington

Introduction

Canada's official policies of bilingualism and multiculturalism have changed little over the past 40 years, but the practices they have fostered have created a conundrum for urban schools. Whereas educational policy in Ontario mandates education in the official languages of English and French, the percentage of children in the Toronto District School Board (TDSB) who speak a language other than English or French at home exceeds 50 per cent,[1] making minorities the majority population, and the linguistically heterogeneous classroom the norm. In English medium classrooms across the Greater Toronto Area (GTA), the majority of learners walk into bilingual learning on school entry in that they enter school with a home language that differs from the language of schooling. They then progress to multilingual learning with the systematic inclusion of French as a second language throughout the English medium school system. The lack of bridges to support learners in their complex language development is a problem.

Education in Canada is provincially rather than nationally governed. The school system mandates a curriculum for children across the province, not just for the greater urban area of Toronto, with which this chapter is concerned. Schooling is thus not geared to the superdiverse population of the GTA, and children and parents alike find themselves having to leave their home language at the school doorstep for an English language environment that does little of substance to welcome their linguistic and cultural knowledge, despite the rhetoric of the multiculturalism policy. To provide a more welcoming and supportive environment for children to become socialized to the official languages of the classroom while learning about and sharing their home languages, we created a learning community for developing multiliteracies pedagogies at Joyce Public School in north-western Toronto. We began by having children revise and retell traditional stories in multimedia forms.

Our solution to the discontinuities in home–school communication was a postmodern proposal: to include the languages of the classroom in multiliteracies projects without unsettling the systemic programming of English and French. This we achieved through a project-based education model centring on narrative learning and multimedia play, which required reconfiguring the school timetable, traditionally sliced into discrete subjects, towards cross-curricular, cross-age literacy projects, where the languages of the children (and teachers) would be welcomed in learning and in textual design.

We developed a learning community with schoolteachers and university researchers at its core, but also involving student teachers, school administrators and guests who were interested in our project. Our mission was to think about contemporary ways of telling stories that were infused with curricular learning. We fitted two lenses on our collaborative action research: plurilingualism and digital play. Intrinsic to these lenses were evolving conceptions of linguistically inclusive education, multimodality, digital literacies and participatory learning.

The teachers relied on both the physical and the digital community to support linguistic pluralism in the classroom. Plurilingual communication was invited in structured educational spaces, processes and products via multimedia and shared learning. Researchers, teachers and children learned in parallel.

The strength of the collaborative planning process to customize stories grew as the learning community developed, sparking adventurous plurilingual projects that involved children of varying ages, and promoting intellectual as well as linguistic development. The children's participation was exciting and sometimes quite surprising, even to the teachers themselves. This chapter describes how we went from disillusionment over an inadequate policy for language and literacy education in a culturally diverse urban society to a DIY approach to linguistically inclusive multimodal literature.

Context

The Greater Toronto Area is a fast-growing urban sprawl listed in the top five largest conurbations in North America. The city of Toronto is the largest in Canada, and is the seat of government for the province of Ontario. The northwestern quadrant of the city of Toronto is the context for the research reported here. The school is Joyce Public School (JPS),[2] which is an elementary school (from kindergarten to Grade 6) in the TDSB catering to a low-income population of high cultural diversity in a community largely constituted of recent migrants to Canada.

Education in Canada is provincially governed, although guided by national priorities. The national English–French bilingualism policy is well known, as are long-established models for French immersion schooling. In Ontario, English and French are the languages officially permitted as media of instruction in public schools, which are attended by over 90 per cent of the population (Van Pelt *et al.*, 2007). Additionally, there are options to study particular international languages as subjects in secondary school, and indigenous languages in specific contexts, as well as extracurricular opportunities to learn/support *heritage languages,* now formally referred to as international languages.

These after-school and weekend programmes emerged in response to Canada's groundbreaking multiculturalism policy but have been subject to changing fortunes and eroding budgets. There are a few urban programmes featuring content-based international language teaching, particularly in the Toronto District Catholic School Board, but these are rare.

English as a second language (ESL) support suffers from continually shrinking budgets, and as such is provided for only a limited segment of the student population – well below need (People for Education, 2012). In any given year, the number of children who are English language learners (ELL) at JPS makes up around two-thirds of the school population, although everyone in the school is at some stage of learning English. Arguably children in the primary grades are also still acquiring their home language/s, given that children enter junior kindergarten at the age of 4. Therefore, virtually all students are in need of English language support. However, the limited budgets for ESL instruction in the TDSB cannot cope with increasing demands, given that over half of all children in Toronto public schools speak a language other than English or French at home, so only a small proportion of children receive pull-out ESL assistance. This means that every classroom teacher is a teacher of English.

Challenges in language and literacy education

Ontario schoolchildren live and learn in a testing culture. Having said that, Ontario students fared among the very top scorers in the 2009 PISA results, according to the province's official testing authority, the Education and Quality Accountability Office (EQAO), which mandatorily tests all students in Ontario at Grades 3, 6, 9 and 10 for literacy and mathematical learning.

High PISA scores are reassuring to policymakers and testers, but they mask a number of problems. Blanket test results provide the illusion that students do not need specialized help or support with languages, including English. However, this is not what has been found in detailed studies of

English language learners' performance in the consequential Ontario Secondary School Literacy Test (OSSLT) administered by the EQAO (Kim and Jang, 2009; Han and Cheng, 2011).

Moreover, the concept of literacy embedded within the EQAO is narrow and outdated, amounting to reading and writing (their conception of) standard English on paper. Kim and Jang's (2009) fine-grained content analysis of the OSSLT locates six subskills in the conception of reading: textual comprehension skill, inferencing skill, vocabulary knowledge, grammatical knowledge, summary skill and integrated reading and writing skill. Although these aims pinpoint important skills in a cognitive conception of literacy, they do not begin to take into consideration the socially embedded nature of literacy, the complex cultural context of literacy practices, the multimodality of digitally mediated communication or the breadth of linguistic diversity in urban classrooms.

The limited concept of literacy in mandatory, high-stakes tests of language and literacy encapsulates the problem we faced in initially thinking about literacy education in the twenty-first century: curricular and assessment aims are out-of-step, oriented to twentieth-century literacy norms, educational models and school populations. Teachers educate students for tomorrow, not yesterday. Though communication builds on historically sedimented practices that we needed to attend to carefully, we were keen to open the view of literacy to one consistent with the student body we were actively working with in the urban elementary school classroom. Our aim, stimulated at the turn of this century by the call to action made by the New London Group (1996) to design a pedagogy of multiliteracies, was to design (multi)literacies pedagogies in step with contemporary social media for our superdiverse student population.

The fulcrum for our explorations was the story: what would a classic folk tale look and sound like revised by the children of today?

Mirror, mirror on the wall: Stories and learning

What is a story? What are the stories we tell children?

Narratives are a major social genre that permeates learning environments from the classroom to the pulpit. Children's literature is a crucial route to literacy development. Decades ago Heath (1982) made the point that the traditional bedtime story prepared middle-class children for school literacy achievement. Reading stories to and with children continues to be routinely recommended in preparation for school literacy learning today.

Traditional children's stories are deeply embedded in common social knowledge. This of course echoes the original intent of the folk tale: to instruct – though the instruction was originally intended for adults (Zipes, 2007). Fables teach through the anthropomorphized animal kingdom: the three little pigs, the big bad wolf, the little red hen, the three bears and the rest of the menagerie inhabiting the pages of fables and folk tales didactically illuminate human foibles.

The European children's canon has even seeped into scientific metaphor: the Goldilocks principle, for instance, taken from the traditional tale of 'Goldilocks and the Three Bears', refers to the happy medium of an activity zone whether in astrobiology or economics. Likewise, the material constructions of the piglets in 'The Three Little Pigs' can be used to refer to choices in investment strategies with the aim of financial stability – to keep the wolf from the door.

Traditional tales have shifted and transformed in both content and form over time. Until the advent of print, stories were malleable: the storyteller could customize the tale to the audience. The publishing industry fixed travelling stories on to a storybook page, cementing characters in the public imagination. These narratives mutated culturally in their transposition from storybook to animated film (and sometimes back into books adapted from the film versions), giving voices as well as shapes to familiar story characters.

Stories have been communicated as oral, dramatized and musical performances; storybooks and print texts; audio-recorded and film versions; video games and fan fiction websites; and in multimedia commodities. Versions of favourite traditional stories treasured in families today were likely encountered in different media by each generation: animated films and spin-off multimedia commodities for children; animated films and picture books for parents; and storybooks for grandparents. To the children of today, accustomed to the mammoth Disney enterprise that fractures narratives across 'TV, toys, fast-food packaging, video games, T-shirts, shoes, bed linen, pencil cases, and lunch boxes' (New London Group, 1996: 70), the Little Mermaid speaks American English, even though Hans Christian Andersen's 'Den lille havfrue' was Danish.

When I first presented the idea of having children revise traditional tales using contemporary digital media to the principal of JPS in 2002/3, we chose 'Goldilocks and the Three Bears'. Interestingly, the idea of changing a fond childhood character met a note of emotional protest from a teacher of Asian descent, for whom Goldilocks was untouchably blonde. The storybook character had represented Canada to this teacher who had arrived in the country as a child from a war-torn country. Why did we have to change an iconic figure? This comment led to a study of Goldilocks's evolution (Lotherington, 2011), which outlined a dramatic metamorphosis in Goldilocks's becoming, from a Scottish she-fox to a snoopy old British lady to a dark-haired girl to the familiar blonde child in American print versions. The answer: because Goldilocks was overdue for a facelift – in more ways than one.

With the growth of new communications media, where software and now apps (i.e. web-based software for mobile devices) are the new lead pencil, students and teachers can retell stories in customizable multimedia, moving back to the idea of the storyteller adapting the story to the audience. The story thus becomes mobile: tailored to particular needs. Our audience was a superdiverse urban classroom in which children spoke a plethora of languages. Given the media to personalize a story, we decided to try out the idea of adapting traditional stories using multimedia, enabling schoolchildren to take an active part in the narrative by tweaking it to their perspective.

This idea, which was in its infancy in 2002/3, proved to be predictive of a much larger social trend in *transmedia* storytelling, described by Jenkins (2006: 220–1) as a 'new aesthetic that has emerged in response to media convergence – one that places new demands on consumers and depends on the active participation of knowledge communities'. Interestingly, Jenkins notes that transmedia storytelling is not new, having been the essence of, for example, Christian storytelling in the Middle Ages in which Jesus is encountered in media such as stained glass windows and tapestries, as well as in sermons and psalms, each assuming prior audience familiarity (Jenkins, 2006: 119). We were aiming for a more coherent meshing of media as a multimedia story, which, nonetheless, pulled the essence of reading and story from the pages of a book as the sole legitimate repository.

We embarked on an experimental journey to retell canonical children's stories in multimedia with the intention of including the children's languages – somehow.

Putting ideas into practice

It is one thing to have a brave new idea about teaching language and literacy using contemporary media, and another thing to translate this into classroom practice. I discussed my idea to revise a familiar folk tale through the children's eyes with the school principal who was keen to exploit the use of new media in the classroom. My aims – admittedly much less coherent then than now – concerned:

1. Literacy acquisition:
    a. Children's engagement with a story could be fundamentally changed if they could edit the story after they read it. Using a digital platform would allow the incipient reader to read/write a story, which is inherently more engaging than learning to read a story fixed in print. Licensed to adapt the story they were learning to read, learners would be swept into the narrative. This would foster deeper textual comprehension, as well as agency in literacy learning.
    b. Stories retold using digital media could employ a suite of communicative modalities, including illustrations, animations, voice-over and music. This would involve learners in multimedia composition – learning to express themselves in multiple modalities, consistent with today's communicative possibilities. It would also provide a supportive buffer to expression, allowing English language learners to lean on their stronger abilities in storytelling.
2. English language acquisition:
    a. Most of the children at JPS not only fell outside the limited bracket of special help with English that the school could provide – they were emblematic of the entire education system. All children needed ELL support, and all classroom teachers had to be able to support them. The idea of recreating stories using multimedia provided children with alternative and complementary expressive avenues for making meaning that augmented their abilities to express themselves, and gave them opportunities to learn English situationally.
3. Plurilingual development:
    a. Although the vague idea of including multiple languages in customized texts was at the root of my initial ideas, the development and formation of plurilingual spaces in multimodal texts was only a hazy shadow at the time. As the years progressed it became focused as a powerful tool in both learning and text production. Its humble beginnings took the shape of wanting to provide children with a linguistic bridge from home to school: to provide spaces for them to incorporate home language knowledge to support ELL development, which is a well-established connection in the research literature (Cummins, 1981; Cummins, 1991; Cummins, 2000; Thomas and Collier, 2001), as well as their complex cultural realities that were so easily diminished in the immigrant story.
    b. On a deeper level, I was interested in building linguistic bridges for two-way language education:

i. to welcome home language knowledge into the classroom to help support children's plurilingual development; but also

ii. to make school learning more accessible to parents, whose collaboration was essential in supporting home language learning.

I was not too sure how this complex vision of literacy learning would work, but the idea of making academic walls more porous to school communities, and responsive to changing social and linguistic realities, was deeply embedded in initial theorizing. The principal liked the idea of experimenting with new pedagogies to help students learn to read and learn English, and making their learning more accessible to parents. She drummed up a group of teachers who volunteered to meet with me after school to hash over my ideas. I presented a broad if somewhat inchoate plan to rewrite traditional children's stories using new media to facilitate language learning and literacy acquisition, and we boldly jumped off a cliff into unknown territory – together.

Two heads are better than one: Creating a culture of collaborative learning

The after-school meetings of that first pilot year (2002/3) formed the initial foundation of a *learning community*, which was a platform for bringing theory and practice together. Our learning community developed over the years from a small after-school interest group into regular monthly workshops scheduled into the school day. We grew from a few curious teachers with the principal and myself to a collective that included two university researchers, numerous graduate students, student teachers and a couple of TDSB specialists, along with the principal and all interested teachers.

What became colloquially known to the teachers as *the multiliteracies project* moved dimensionally from early baffled questions from the teachers as to what I wanted, what was to be done by Tuesday and when the computer lab was free, to a dialogic forum facilitating participatory action research that was funded by the Social Science and Humanities Research Council of Canada until the end of 2012.[3] Regular workshops evolved into a planning and sharing process through which our common pursuit of new pedagogies for new literacies provided professional development catering to the teachers' classes, interests and issues, while informing our action research agenda (see Lotherington, 2011; Lotherington *et al.*, 2013). During a decade of continuous research, I became an insider to the school: an active participant rather than an academic observer. This gave me an *emic* perspective (Fetterman, 2008) in an ethnographic voyage to bring together theory and practice in the development of new pedagogies for language and literacy education in linguistically complex urban classrooms.

What *multiliteracies* meant was part of our exploration. Teachers were invited to focus on any part of new literacies that interested them given our research parameters of linguistic inclusion, multimedia expression and digital play. Some concentrated on digital literacies; some, cultural sharing; others, inviting home languages into learning practices. As we became experienced participants in a learning community, teachers' particular interests and levels of expertise were shared across the group. Their ideas, plans, problems and successes motivated increasingly adventurous collaborations and complex learning that entwined plurilingualism and digital expression.

New old stories: Culture shock

Class projects began as children's multimedia retelling of a selected traditional story. We began with the story of 'Goldilocks and the Three Bears', with the objective of documenting how children would write themselves into the narrative (see Lotherington and Chow, 2006). Would Goldilocks speak another language? Might she be a boy instead of a girl? Could she – or he – have brown skin or black hair? Might Goldilocks become Dreadlocks?

The first run of children's revised narratives was inspiring, if a bit twisted up in knots. Two things stood out:

- The pervasiveness of Disney branding was evident in the children's reproduced storybook characters. Cultural theorists, such as Giroux (2010) and Dorfman (2010), critique the insidiousness of the stereotypes created in the Disney (and in others') cartoon empires. Numerous protagonists of traditional folk and fairy tales, such as the Little Mermaid, Cinderella, Snow White and Ali Baba, have been given a Disney makeover, trademarked and stamped onto commodities, from bed sheets to book bags. Children knew these characters, but not necessarily their narrative contexts.
- Children had difficulties stringing together coherent plots. This indicated how difficult a story actually is, which presented teachers with a scaffolding agenda.

The teachers had already suggested that the world of digital pop culture forged a sense of shared culture for students. My expectations that the heritage culture of the home would drive children's cultural retellings missed an obvious point: communication was changing in the rapidly digitizing social sphere, and so was culture. Children were becoming acculturated into a Disneyesque world. And in Disney's world, the characters spoke English – all of them.

Take two on Goldilocks included more teachers in the primary grades of kindergarten–Grade 2, and the addition of other traditional stories: 'The Little Red Hen', 'The Gingerbread Man' and 'The Three Little Pigs'. Story grammars took visual shape on screens for the children. The kindergarten teacher sculpted the linear narrative trajectory as a title–beginning–middle–end curve to help children picture title, set-up, problem and denouement. The Grade 2 teacher worked on character, plot and setting in her teaching, focusing children on adapting only character and/or setting, but not the fundamental plot. This way, children knew what could be changed. As characters morphed, their settings changed, and the results by far exceeded any estimation of what I thought children might imagine by jumping into the main protagonist's head.

New old stories: Crowdsourcing linguistic resources

Jenkins (2006: 21) describes transmedia stories as involving 'the active participation of knowledge communities'. We used crowdsourcing to support linguistic customization in children's stories, which we discovered in the local as well as in the digital community.

With the visual presentation of a storyline, small children had numerous overlapping semiotic resources available to them: pictures, words in letters and in sounds, music and animation, though not all resources were used, or used simultaneously. Early bilingual versions of retold stories tapped the knowledge of people at school: the teachers and teaching assistants. Mike created a trilingual English, Cantonese and Vietnamese word wall of 'The Little Red Hen', drawing on the languages spoken by the educational assistants in his junior/senior kindergarten (4–5 year olds). The three linguistic versions were pegged to picture placeholders of story characters: the hen, the pig and the dog (see Figure 5.1). This allowed children multiple entry points to the story: from Cantonese, Vietnamese or English. Not only did the children in his class become more curious about everyone's languages, but sharing the numbers from 1 to 10 in home languages became a competitive oral activity. Mike also noted that children's parents were curious about the languages, shyly emerging from the doorways to comment.

Mike Zentena, Joyce Public School

Figure 5.1: 'The Little Red Hen' trilingual word wall in Mike's kindergarten

Teachers also crowdsourced translations from home. Shiva invited the parents of children in her Grade 1 class to help out with oral translations of their children's rewritten stories of 'The Three Little Pigs', creating the framework for movies of the children's animated PowerPoints that had multiple soundtracks, tailored to the language profiles of participating children. In this plan, languages were stackable. English and the home language were available in different modalities: one in print, which was always there, and another in sound with on–off options. We ran into a snag, however, trying to programme well-meaning translations as parallel soundtracks, given that teachers did not know the home languages. How were they to decide where the spoken translations matched the English text?

Michelle, a kindergarten teacher, hit on a fundamental fix: she co-programmed two languages into one version of her learners' retold stories of 'The Lion and the Mouse' with the help of the educational assistant who had provided the translation. The essential role of collaboration in our project thus grew in scope: retold multimedia stories were group efforts from their conception to their realization. They had to be programmed in sync by those contributing (see Lotherington *et al.* (2008) for more on these three teachers' early multiliteracies projects).

The brick and mortar school was becoming less and less a frontier, walling languages in and out, as parents felt more confidence entering the grounds, and contributing to their own and other people's children's learning. This principle was further extended when I suddenly realized that we had endless translations of anything we wanted using digital resources. This great idea was shot down just as rapidly when we tried out machine translations in our learning community with languages we could understand, revealing hopelessly mangled, tragically funny translations. With today's much more accurate online language help, digital translation might no longer be the hit-and-miss proposition it was a decade ago. But the answer we needed at the time was right in front of our eyes: to connect with people via digital pathways.

A former JPS teacher who had moved to Taiwan with her family came to us requesting a collaborative link. Using free digital connections such as Skype, we began a remote school collaboration with a private school in Taipei.

Creating spaces for plurilingualism in the urban elementary classroom

By 2008 our learning community had grown to include a fellow professor, an expert in pedagogy and technology, Professor Jennifer Jenson, who added a ludic, or game-playing, perspective to plurilingualism. This strengthened our knowledge about merging languages in multimedia texts both pedagogically and technically. Our project, which had begun with primary grade teachers working with language and literacy acquisition through the multimedia retelling of canonical children's stories, had begun to attract junior grade (4–5) teachers as well.

The projects had become more complex in construction and implementation, stretching goals across social studies, English, music and science in complex multiclass projects. In the primary sector, Michelle and Sonia designed a kindergarten–Grade 2 collaboration around 'The Three Billy Goats Gruff' to teach anti-bullying strategies. Children's collaborative narratives rewrote the goats, and particularly the troll, to be polite and respectful. The stories were then grouped by children's home languages and translated with the assistance of members of the school community who had a written knowledge of Cantonese, Turkish and a number of other languages. The bilingual narratives were developed into playscapes that the children created and acted out, complete with costumes, set design and narrator. These were photographed and inserted into their retold storybooks. The culminating activity was a pizza night at the school when parents and children came together and completed children's revised bilingual storybooks in family groupings, customizing story endings (see Figure 5.2, and see Lotherington *et al.* (2013) for more details).

Heather Lotherington, York University

Figure 5.2: Parent and kindergartner customizing her bilingual retold 'Three Billy Goats Gruff' story

In the junior panel, a large consortium of teachers had chosen the story of 'Cinderella', which they tied to self-concept and skin-deep visual beauty (no thanks to Disney), invoking issues of racial and gender stereotypes and body dysmorphia. The project group drew on the human senses in the science curriculum, each teacher tackling one of the five most commonly reported human senses with the aim of discovering what was beautiful to students in each sense domain. I must admit to attending as many classes as possible to enjoy teachers' creative activities experimenting with sensory channels, which included a brutal taste-test of unsweetened chocolate, listening to children describe how their dog smells, and watching pre-teens make abstract finger paintings.

In Rhea's class, the children (all facing learning challenges) focused on getting below superficial ideals of beauty in individual multimedia projects about what was personally beautiful to each child. Projects incorporated 3D artwork and a written description in English and the home language, including Caribbean Creoles, which we insisted on assigning equal space in the classroom. These were digitized into portfolios including pictures of the children.

At the culminating gallery walk, I talked to children informally about their *beauty* projects portraying such objects as their favourite sports shoes, African drum, rock guitar and snow globe (see Figure 5.3). A number of children read their project descriptions to me in languages such as Tamil and Guyanese Creole. Rhea described how multifaceted the project of multisensory engagement was, recalling one task where children were asked to free draw to a variety of types of music in a moment of synaesthetic engagement. Interestingly, the learning-challenged students happily started in on the task, whereas top students had difficulties, asking what the teacher expected in the final product. One of the strengths of our multiliteracies project was in moving children away from *getting the right answer* into a realm of discovery where they framed personal responses using the languages and communications media to which they had access (see Lotherington and Sinitskaya Ronda (2012) for further details).

Heather Lotherington, York University
Figure 5.3: Snow globes

A very beautiful talking book was created at the junior level in another complex multi-teacher consortium working with the notion of respect in describing common humanity. This project was a precursor to health and science discussions about differences in human behaviour, focusing on sexual orientation and anti-homophobia. *Imagine a World* engaged plurilingualism in its essence: the children created the images and wrote the text; they sourced the myriad translations used alongside the continuous English text, and spoke the multilingual soundtrack in the talking book (see Figure 5.4).[4]

Andrew Schmitt, Joyce Public School

Figure 5.4: A page from the collaboratively created talking book: *Imagine a World*

These short vignettes of multiliteracies projects engaging students' and teachers' home languages planned, developed and implemented in classrooms by members of our learning community showcase discursive and textual spaces for plurilingual engagement. Students' home languages were invited into primary classroom talk around familiar tasks such as answering morning roll call, making greetings and learning base numbers, though this usage is primarily displaying knowledge rather than learning the language or engaging intellectually with content provided in it. Textual spaces included customized bilingual and trilingual print media; multimodal incorporation of languages customized to children's language profiles (L1 written text – L2 soundtrack); and plurilingual texts, such as *Imagine a World*, where the many languages contributed by children ran ad hoc alongside English, such that no one individual could read the entire text. However, the class could read it aloud collaboratively because each child could interpret the translation he or she had contributed to the whole text. The message of the whole text is clear even if each line is not readable to every reader as there is a constant English thread. The multimodal, multilingual resources used in the construction of the talking book respect the contributions of each participant: a true collaborative piece.

Conclusion: A DIY approach to creating plurilingual literature

Where is the beginning or end of an idea and how can we express it? Halliday (1993: 93) states, 'the prototypical form of human semiotic is language', the development of which is continuous learning though it be multidimensional in expressive modes and domains.

In this day and age, the borders of language and languages are becoming increasingly nebulous. Creating a plurilingual classroom means confronting boundaries that have become sedimented in linguistic and educational thinking: Where do languages begin and end? Where does language competence begin and end? What languages are taught and used and to what purpose in the classroom? What languages are excluded and why? Where do we find common ground in communication? How are the edges of language blending with other semiotic forms?

With each annual cycle, our learning community grew in acumen and courage. The principal – a visionary leader – was a strong supporting force in this development: she believed in research-based teaching, and supported creative risk-taking that had students' advancement and well-being at its core. How important this attitude is cannot be overemphasized. Virtually nothing we planned worked as anticipated the first time around, though there were always indications of how we could work with problems to move forward. This was the essence of progress in participatory action research: moving one step back to every two ahead in the pursuit of linguistically enriching, digitally immersive pedagogies.

The principal's high expectations were borne out. By the time our research funding had come to an end in 2012, JPS students' scores on mandatory EQAO tests of reading and writing had risen dramatically despite the fact that we studiously avoided the coaching mentality to cognitive skills-based learning that these tests of individual performance encouraged, and even though the limited ESL assistance available in the school and high percentage of ELL had not changed.

My interpretation of children's improved test scores owes a great deal to the idea of agency in learning. Children needed to be given permission to express themselves in different languages. They had to see the value in this and to develop the courage to participate by communicating with parents and teachers and each other across a spectrum of languages. They had contemporary (though hardly state-of-the-art) communications media available to them, and the licence to be creative, though they also had specific curricular and narrative goals. There was no right answer in retold stories; no moment when students were wrong. Figuring out who was best at what and how they could share their skills to best effect in narrative creation buried the idea of getting the right answer. Importantly, having home languages to share in the classroom-supported home–school communication and intergenerational learning, and contributed to an anti-racist classroom in which students realized that difference might just be cool. It was certainly a commonality.

Although we succeeded in experimentally building DIY plurilingual literature in the urban elementary classroom, not all aims were equally met. We succeeded at:

- creating a model learning community which functioned beautifully (after it got going) as a planning and implementation body for developing new pedagogies: a DIY in-school think tank
- breaking down school and intergenerational walls for the flow of community-based languages into and out of the classroom
- creating discursive and textual spaces for plurilingualism in original, creative and fulfilling ways that children were proud to take a part in.

Grade 4/5 teacher Andrew expresses the children's growing confidence in expressing themselves plurilingually, re: *Imagine a World*:

> I think the scope and the scale of that project is, was the remarkable part about it, and yeah, it was just really neat to uh, to get the kids to be able to say, uh, to hear their voices, and to see their artwork and put the two together, get their home languages in there. And then one of the big moments for me was showing a draft of it to the kids, where it was like, you know, 43 per cent complete, and having all these kids come back and say 'I want to do it, I want to be a part of it', that hadn't wanted to, that went home and got translations to come back so that they could add that dimension of it as well to their part and that was, and that to me, was fascinating, because it was like: you know, we're trying to do this, we're trying to do it but, it wasn't until they saw it and heard it and felt it that they realized that this was something they wanted to be part of.

However, our use of multiple languages in the classroom relied largely on translation, which limited the scope for language learning and maintenance in the classroom, despite supporting language appreciation and anti-racism. Effectively opening up two-way home–school bridges for language maintenance was elusive, and, worse, with successive years we had to work harder and harder to convince parents who were hell-bent on their children learning English and French that their home languages were valuable. We still have much work to do to educate the general population about the fact that we live in global times where national language borders no longer delimit expertise in communication.

At the end of the research funding I left the school quietly, having become superfluous to the functioning of the learning community. Though I felt sad to leave, I realized that this was a resounding testament to the success of our venture. The learning community had slowly undergone a maturation process culminating in its becoming a fundamental part of school culture. Teachers requested permission of the principal to pool their prep times so they could organize collegial workshops during which they could continue to plan and conduct cross-curricular, cross-age projects that enfolded selected elements of the mandated curriculum as well as bringing in the language knowledge of the class, and engaging a variety of media – digital and other – to build agentive multimedia projects with a plurilingual mindset.

Notes

[1] www.tdsb.on.ca/AboutUs/QuickFacts.aspx.

[2] Permission to use the school's and the teachers' real names was sought in the ethical reviews of this SSHRC-funded collaborative action research project (reviewed by the Toronto District School Board and York University) in response to a request for non-anonymity from the school.

[3] I owe my sincere gratitude to SSHRC for their support of our collaborative action research at Joyce Public School.

[4] The talking book, *Imagine a World*, can be accessed at: www.youtube.com/watch?v=8zabcX_zoP0.

References

Cummins, J. (1981) *Bilingualism and Minority Language Children*. Toronto, ON: Ontario Institute for Studies in Education of the University of Toronto.

— (1991) 'Interdependence of first- and second-language proficiency'. In Bialystok, E. (ed.) *Language Processing in Bilingual Children*. Cambridge: Cambridge University Press, 70–89.

— (2000) *Language, Power and Pedagogy: Bilingual children in the crossfire*. Clevedon: Multilingual Matters.

Dorfman, A. (2010) *The Empire's Old Clothes: What the Lone Ranger, Babar, and other innocent heroes do to our minds*. Durham, NC: Duke University Press.

Fetterman, D.F. (2008) 'Emic/etic distinction'. In Given, L.M. (ed.) *The Sage Encyclopedia of Qualitative Research Methods* (Vol. 2). Los Angeles, CA: Sage, 70–89.

Giroux, H.A. (2010) *The Mouse that Roared: Disney and the end of innocence*. Blue Ridge Summit, PA: Rowman and Littlefield.

Halliday, M.A.K. (1993) 'Towards a language-based theory of learning'. *Linguistics and Education*, 5 (2), 93–116.

Han, H. and Cheng, L. (2011) 'Tracking the success of English language learners within the context of the Ontario Secondary School Literacy Test'. *Canadian and International Education/Education canadienne et internationale*, 40 (1), 76–96. Online. http://ir.lib.uwo.ca/cie-eci/vol40/iss1/6 (accessed 6 June 2014).

Heath, S.B. (1982) 'What no bedtime story means: Narrative skills at home and school'. *Language and Society*, 11 (2), 49–76.

Jenkins, H. (2006) *Convergence Culture: Where old and new media collide*. New York: New York University Press.

Kim, Y-H. and Jang, E. (2009) 'Differential functioning of reading subskills on the OSSLT for L1 and ELL students: A multidimensionality model-based DBF/DIF approach'. *Language Learning*, 59 (4), 825–65.

Lotherington, H. (2011) *Pedagogy of Multiliteracies: Rewriting Goldilocks*. New York: Routledge.

Lotherington, H. and Chow, S. (2006) 'Rewriting Goldilocks in the urban, multicultural elementary school'. *The Reading Teacher*, 60 (3), 244–52.

Lotherington, H., Paige, C. and Holland-Spencer, M. (2013) 'Using a professional learning community to support multimodal literacies'. *What works? Research into Practice*. Toronto: Literacy and Numeracy Secretariat. Online. www.edu. gov.on.ca/eng/literacynumeracy/inspire/research/WW_Professional_Learning.pdf (accessed 6 June 2014).

Lotherington, H. and Sinitskaya Ronda, N. (2012) 'Revisiting communicative competence in the multimedia ELT classroom'. In Li, J. and Edwards, N. (eds) *Video Digital Media in the TESOL Classroom*. Alexandria, VA: TESOL International Association, 9–32.

Lotherington, H., Sotoudeh, S., Holland, M. and Zentena, M. (2008) 'Project-based community language learning: Three narratives of multilingual storytelling in early childhood education'. *Canadian Modern Language Review*, 65 (1), 125–45.

New London Group (1996) 'A pedagogy of multiliteracies: Designing social factors'. *Harvard Educational Review*, 66 (1), 60–92.

People for Education (2012) *Support for Newcomer Students*. Online. www. peopleforeducation.ca/wp-content/uploads/2013/01/support-for-newcomer-students.pdf (accessed 6 June 2014).

Thomas, W.P. and Collier, V.P. (2001) *A National Study of School Effectiveness for Language Minority Students' Long-Term Academic Achievement*. Berkeley, CA: Center for Research on Education, Diversity & Excellence.

Van Pelt, D.A., Allison, P.A. and Allison, D.J. (2007) *Ontario's Private Schools: Who chooses them and why?* Studies in Education Policy. The Fraser Institute. Online. www.fraserinstitute.org/research-news/display.aspx?id=13269 (accessed 6 June 2014).

Zipes, J.D. (2007) *When Dreams Came True: Classical fairy tales and their tradition*. 2nd edn. New York: Routledge.

Chapter 6

Interweaving cultures through bilingual fairy tales[1]

A communitarian programme linking family and school literacy practices

Judith Oller

Introduction

Large-scale international studies evaluating the academic performance of immigrant students indicate that the social and cultural features of their families are relevant to their results at school (OECD, 2006). Households that stimulate literacy activities at home and promote the development of academic skills in the language of instruction enhance the performance of their children. The reality in Spain, however, is that many immigrant parents maintain their native languages only at home, and mostly in oral activities, so that knowledge of heritage languages fades in the second and following generations.

Moreover, African parents in Spain are often encumbered by the idea of linguistic, cultural or social deficit, especially the women who are responsible for educating and raising their children. Such ideas have different origins. Many teachers regard African women as illiterate, traditional, authoritarian or unconcerned about their children's performance at school and believe that African families should delegate their educational function to the school. In addition, stereotypical views and prejudices prevail about immigrant students and their families at school, especially about groups perceived as more distant from the national 'norm' such as families from Africa.

Actis (2004), who studied teachers' discourses about cultural diversity in Spain regarding immigrant ethnic minorities, found that most professionals considered the presence of immigrant students at school a 'major problem'. Some teachers argue that the root of the problem lies in the immigrant students themselves – poor study habits, lack of proficiency in the second language, negative attitudes, lack of involvement in schoolwork – whereas others attribute failure to the families. Immigrant families, especially Muslims, are seen as:

demotivated, with no interest in school or without time to spend on the education of their children, and with cultural practices and values which make schoolwork difficult (in addition to the idiomatic gaps in the language of instruction, they rely on their authoritarianism over children and their deceit with institutions).

(Actis, 2004: 15; trans. Judith Oller)

Notions about the deficiencies of immigrant families often present groups as homogeneous and thus nurture stereotyped views (Ortiz, 2008). Disinformation about immigrant parents and their educational activities often inhibits the establishment of mutual trust between them and the school, especially with regard to literacy practices. Some cultural activities at home are not seen as valuable resources, and schools often try to replace them with more 'appropriate' occidental literacy practices, creating asymmetrical relationships that can depress immigrant children's school performance (Gregory and Williams, 2000). Clarke *et al.* (2010) point out that good relationships between schools and families depend on confidence, mutual sensitivity and equal distribution of power, so the school must be open to diversity, recognize its limitations and take advantage of the resources that families and communities can provide.

In this chapter I describe an innovative research action project that seeks to promote educational continuities between the literacy practices of immigrant African groups in Catalonia and those of schools. The project aims to make visible immigrant families' funds of knowledge (Vélez-Ibáñez and Greenberg, 1992), especially their literacy activities in their heritage languages (L1), through the development of bilingual storybooks in Catalan and their L1. Suggestions are offered about how to expand and develop communitarian projects and embed them into the school culture.

Interweaving Cultures Project – *El projecte Teixint Cultures*

In October 2009 I started a communitarian project in a public library that aimed to empower African immigrant mothers' literacy practices in their L1 and use their linguistic and cultural resources to bridge activities in school and home. The ongoing programme is being conducted in Salt (Girona), a city that has one of the largest proportions of immigrants in Spain (about 42 per cent of the total population). Salt hosts people from more than 40 countries of origin, who speak over 65 different languages. The schools average over 80 per cent immigrant students, and there is a large incidence of academic failure among them, especially those of African or Asian background. Many programmes to promote the academic success of immigrant children have been developed by the central administration, the local council and several non-governmental organizations. Their goal of social cohesion is far from being reached, as it is difficult to involve immigrant families in local and school activities.

The project is run under the auspices of the GRAMC social association (Grups de Recerca i Acció amb Minories Culturals, www. gramc.org) in collaboration with the research group Cultura i Educació from the University of Girona and members of the public library in Salt. The Interweaving Cultures Project assumes that all families have useful educational resources to promote children's development and that these funds of knowledge constitute the basis of the families' social capital and are valuable educational resources for use in school. Reviving African traditional fairy tales, groups of immigrant women (assisted by community volunteers) are collaborating in the creation of bilingual storybooks in their L1 and Catalan, for use as educational resources in the public library, at home and in local schools.

This innovative project in the field of adult education promotes educational continuities between the literacy practices developed for immigrant children at home and school. The project aims to empower the literacy competence of immigrant families using their own linguistic resources; to promote educational continuities between home and school literacy activities; and to revalue the importance of heritage languages and the culture of minority students at school and in society.

The theoretical and ideological ideas underlying the project

The Interweaving Cultures Project arose from the need to change the negative perception of immigrant minority groups living in Catalonia, especially those from African countries, and restore the importance of heritage languages for linguistic and identity reasons. I have noted that immigrant families are seen as having poor linguistic and educational resources. For example, Gabrielli (2010) found that Senegalese and Gambian parents are stereotyped in Catalonia as homogeneous groups that are 'illiterate', 'traditional', 'slightly authoritarian' and, in some senses, 'unconcerned about their children's academic results'. Moroccan groups face historical prejudice against their language, culture and religion (see Colectivo Ioé, 2007).

Consequently, many teachers assume that immigrant students and their families from certain countries need special support to develop their educational role. But most teachers know nothing about the activities in which African immigrant students are involved, whether at home or in their neighbourhoods. Many studies have pointed out that their families' everyday literacy practices are not valued or even considered within the schools. Yet there are many: Gregory *et al.* (2004) cite, for example, Qur'anic study in the mosque or at home, telling traditional fairy tales and legends, seeking information on the internet in L1, viewing television programmes in L1 and consulting cooking recipes written in L1, among many others.

I agree with Vila and Casares (2009) that school culture 'prioritizes' those students and families who share the *savoir faire* that schools consider necessary to promote academic performance, while neglecting or rejecting the educational practices that they consider more 'distant'. The failure of the immigrant students is attributed to the parents' difficulty in promoting the literacy practices necessary for academic success, while the particular learning context is not even considered.

In summary, African immigrant families living in Spain are often perceived as 'deficient' in their education and social capital and their children are forced to assimilate dominant cultural literacy practices and abandon their own. The school practices do not help to create an inclusive environment in which multilingualism and multiculturalism are valued. Innovative initiatives are needed which address the treatment of immigrant students' L1 if we are to take advantage of the richness of African language and culture in Catalonian classrooms and society.

Accordingly, I designed an innovative project in the field of adult education to promote literacy skills, oral and written, in Catalan and the heritage languages of local African mothers in Salt, such as Arabic, Mandingo, Wolof and Soninke. The project is built on three basic pillars: the role of first language (L1) in learning a second language (L2); the need to bridge home and school literacy practices; and the notion of empowerment as a centrepiece of the intervention.

The role of L1 in learning an L2

The right to develop one's mother tongue has been reflected in UNESCO reports since 1953, but even today there are millions of children who follow their studies in a different language from their own. Advocates of bilingual education have shown the importance of first language in the learning of a second language and hence in the academic success of bilingual children (see Baker, 1996). They stress that when minority students can develop their linguistic proficiency in their L1 throughout the compulsory school years their second language proficiency increases considerably – and more quickly than that of students in a transitional programme (Thomas and Collier, 1997).

Cummins (2001) points out that the incorporation of students' L1 affirms and benefits the identity of newcomer students, and shows how it fosters their active participation and involvement in class activities. Consequently the level of L1 academic development is a strong predictor of L2 proficiency (Cummins, 2000). Therefore, teaching methodologies need to use students' L1 as a resource for L2 learning if we are to promote the academic success of all students. And it is important to convince immigrant families to keep their home language as an asset and help them to promote the development of L1, going beyond conversational uses and focusing on the promotion of academic skills to support their children's school activities.

For all these reasons, our project uses the 'dual-language' approach (Lindholm-Leary, 2001) to support biculturalism and promote the development of immigrant mothers' literacy in both L1 and L2. Our methodology develops linguistic skills through the use of content instruction activities in two languages, and promotes multicultural competence for all students.

Taylor *et al*. (2008), for example, reported on the positive effects of using heritage languages to develop linguistic skills and initial literacy in the language of instruction (English) in a Toronto kindergarten in which seven different languages were represented. Students, aged from 3 to 5 years, were involved in the production of bilingual identity texts (in English and their heritage languages) that explained things about their families, themselves or their favourite activities at home and at school. Texts were initially written in English with the support of teachers, and were translated into the heritage language of the children. A 'multiliteracies' approach was used (Cope and Kalantzis, 2000), and children were encouraged to draw pictures to support the text, and also to include family photographs and other symbolic elements. At the end of the year, individual texts were scanned and turned into bilingual books that were made available on the school website to allow other family members living outside Canada to enjoy the material. In this case, the use of the L1 to foster reading and writing in English helped to increase students' self-esteem and their academic performance, as well as parental involvement in their children's multiliterate practices. In addition, the authors state: 'home literacies associated with complex transnational and transgenerational communities of practice were legitimated through their inclusion within the school curriculum' (Taylor *et al*., 2008: 269).

One inspirational programme for the Interweaving Cultures Project was developed in the Thornwood School in Ontario, Canada (Schecter and Cummins, 2003). Immigrant families were invited to create bilingual books in their home language and in the instructional language, English, for use at school. As Cummins later observed, these books and bilingual materials operated as 'identity texts' for immigrant students, engaging them in academic activities and improving communication between their families and their school (Cummins, 2006). Cummins points out that the use of their first language was a tool for improving the students' written productions in English. Moreover, the immigrant parents were actively involved in their children's homework, and knowledge and awareness grew in the school and community of the cultural activities and values reflected in the stories the children built. As the school activities included audio-recorded texts in two languages, students and families with limited English proficiency were able to expand their lexical knowledge and basic grammatical structures in English through comparison of their L1 with the L2.

Bridging home and school literacy practices

Parents who promote literacy and support the development of students' academic skills at home strengthen the school performance of their children (Desforges and Abouchaar, 2003). Not all families' educational practices are valued in the same way at school, however. A major barrier for establishing collaborative spaces between schools and immigrant families is the stereotyping of the immigrant students by schools and the disinformation regarding the cultural and literacy activities developed in the two contexts. Martin-Jones and Jones (2000) compiled several studies on various immigrant groups in England that showed how their schools failed to take any account of the wide linguistic repertoires learned by these children outside the school class. Because their linguistic practices were not visible in the school, teachers suggested educational practices that had little to do with those developed naturally in their cultural activities. In most cases, the ultimate goal of these practices was to replace home activities with others that the schools viewed as more 'standardized' (Gregory *et al.*, 2004).

However, to foster children's development it is necessary to create educational continuities among the contexts in which children actively participate, especially between family and school (Bronfenbrenner, 1979). In particular, when two or more microsystems work together to achieve common educational goals, the educational potential of each is amplified. Since continuity relations are built on mutual trust, reciprocity and recognition of the importance of activities in different contexts (rather than simply doing the same activities at home and school), the first step is to break down the barriers that separate the two contexts.

Our project assumes that all families – whatever their economic status, level of education, structure or organization – have positive educational resources to foster their children's development. The funds of knowledge of immigrant families are enormously diverse and constitute the basis of their social capital (Vélez-Ibáñez and Greenberg, 1992). As González *et al.* (2005) and Martin-Jones and Saxena (2003) state, there is an urgent need for schools to recognize these educational resources in households and use them to foster academic success. Our project aims to recognize and value the cultural and linguistic practices of African immigrant groups and to put them on an equal status with the educational practices that are valued within Western society.

Empowerment

There is much research indicating how social inequalities and coercive power relations are at the root of the poor school performance of minority students (see Cummins (2000) for a review). As Street (1984) notes, literacy practices are not only aspects of culture but also aspects of power structures. Schools often try to reproduce and maintain certain ways of 'legitimate' communication, promoting only literacy practices that are similar to those valued at school, such as storytelling or bedtime reading, and rejecting other literacy practices, especially those from minority students' households, as 'illegitimate' or even 'irrelevant' (Heller and Martin-Jones, 2001).

In our project, African oral traditional fairy tales are recovered and bilingual storybooks are developed. This empowers the immigrant women, assisted by community volunteers, to develop an active role in the promotion of early literacy activities at home, and to actively share their resources with others in the school and local cultural spaces. It is assumed that all participants – volunteers, educators, women and their children – will take an active role in making possible the elaboration of bilingual books. The tasks involved are complex and require two or more participants to work together throughout the different stages of the project. Collaboration is promoted that takes advantage of the funds of knowledge of all the participants and fosters their confidence and self-esteem. The public library where we conduct the project has now become a familiar space in which the participants' social capital is shared, and the creation of social networking with people from different origins is encouraged.

Design of the project and participants

Since October 2009, diverse groups of African women and the children in their charge (under 3 years old) have met once a week for two hours in Salt's public library. The Interweaving Cultures Project started up with one educator, two researchers and five local volunteers. The initial group was composed of ten immigrant women who also attended a course in Catalan as a second language with GRAMC. Now more than 50 participants benefit from the project, most of them from Morocco, Gambia and Senegal.

Most of the women who first participated in the project were young (age 29 on average), multilingual, with children under 3 years old and at least one more attending school, and had recently arrived (between one and two years earlier on average). Many of them had come some years after their husbands to improve their living conditions or because of family reunification. But they had arrived in Spain when the economic crisis bit and unemployment was rising. So most of these families struggled financially and had little contact with local citizens. African women play an important role in the maintenance of their cultural traditions and family values as they care for their children, while the men are responsible for supporting their families. The men learn basic Catalan and Spanish while at work, whereas their wives use the languages they spoke in their countries of origin because they have little contact with people outside their extended family. Their Catalan was too poor for them to communicate effectively in everyday situations like shopping in the supermarket, making an appointment at the town hall or understanding the teachers at a school interview, and they spent most of the day inside their homes.

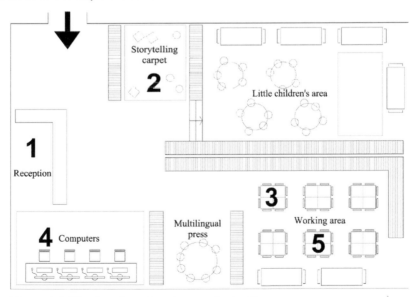

Figure 6.1: The function of each space in the library

The majority of women attending our programme had finished elementary education and begun Catalan courses for adults, but they generally gave up after a few months because they were not allowed to bring their children to the courses. Our project was a response to a widespread need for African immigrant women to find a context in which they could learn Catalan with their children present.

The Interweaving Cultures Project operates in stages. Figure 6.1 shows how the spaces in the library are allotted to the different stages of the programme.

Stage 1: Reception and initial welcome

Volunteers welcome the new participants and their children and take them around the public library, showing them the nursery space, computers, main work-tables, children's literature, multilingual space with journals and newspapers in different minority and international languages, and the space for little children and family activities. They meet the other participants, and the aims of the project and the working procedure are explained. We note their nationality, first language, level of proficiency in Catalan and any other languages, length of residence in Spain, level of education, number of children and age, and their phone number or contact address. Those who are interested in collaborating with us in the elaboration of bilingual materials and learning Catalan join the rest of the group.

Stage 2: Initial routine with children

Before we start work each day, we sit on a large carpet together – the mothers, their little children and an early childhood educator – to sing a song or even tell a story in Catalan. The routine is similar to the activities developed in kindergarten, and aims to facilitate the transition of the children to the local school. At the same time, their mothers can learn a few school activities that could be tried at home and tell us about their own cultural practices. After the joint activity, the educator and volunteers take care of the children in a safe area of the library, while their mothers work in an annexe.

Stage 3: Elaboration of bilingual stories

This phase of the project may last several months. It begins with a participant sharing a fairy tale, legend or story they were told in their L1 in their country of origin. With the help of local bilingual volunteers, usually second generation African migrants, other women and an educator, stories are narrated and shared in Catalan with the whole group. Translanguaging is used to create meaning within the different fairy tales and their content – French and Spanish are used to facilitate translations into Catalan, for example; heritage languages are used to access some lexical roots. We use this activity to talk about the meaning of the stories, the links with their countries of origin and whether the women keep those traditions at home.

We may also talk about the grief that migration can imbue. Then the women work in pairs or small groups, ideally those who share the same L1, but otherwise using a lingua franca, to write their own story in their language. Participants can use any language to communicate with others, but we do encourage the use of Catalan so that they can learn it.

Next, the original story is translated into Catalan. We take advantage of the linguistic resources of all the participants, educators and volunteers because the ultimate goal is to learn Catalan through discussing and comparing words and syntax. We also use the bilingual dictionaries, a thesaurus and online resources in the library. The illiterate women record the story on audio while those who are literate try to write it down.

Stage 4: Editing, illustrating and reviewing the material

Once the stories are written, participants use the library computers to edit the texts. Those who are not familiar with computers receive basic training in word processor programs and basic online applications. To write texts in non-Latin languages such as Arabic we use specific programs from the internet that allow one to type with a different keyboard layout. When the texts are finished, we print out multiple copies and read them aloud. In this phase we work in groups of four or five people to check the accuracy of the translation and the vocabulary used in the L1 and L2. The objective is to create a translation of the text as close as possible to the original. To meet this challenge, the teacher uses various activities to work on the different aspects of the stories: structure, narration process, different ways to start or end a tale and so on. Dramatization is used as a main resource for practice, and we also spend time, during the initial stages, on shared reading between mothers and children. The reviewed texts are illustrated by community volunteers and occasionally by older children attending the library after a storytelling activity the participants have developed.

At the end of the first year of the project, educators and researchers edited a bilingual collection of ten African traditional fairy tales, two of them from Senegal and Gambia written in Catalan–Mandingo, and eight from Morocco and Algeria written in Catalan–Arabic. As the participants were schooled in English and French in their countries of origin, and did not know the grammatical rules of their own language, Mandingo, we decided to use a phonetic translation of the Mandingo words in the Latin alphabet. Arabic texts were written with all the vowels to make reading the book easier for the novice learners. The book includes watercolour drawings of the different characters in the stories painted by a volunteer who is an artist.

Some of the published fairy tales can be accessed online from the project website: http://teixintcultures.wordpress.com/projecte-teixtint-cultures/mostres-de-material/.

Stage 5: Collecting the symbolic world of tales in different cultures

We held discussion sessions about the first collection of stories to bring out the hidden intentions and the morals in them. In these sessions, we asked the participants about their experience of storytelling and story-reading in their countries of origin and the value of tales for transmitting norms, values and attitudes to children. We analysed the symbolism of the main characters in the stories, such as the way they act, the meaning of animals in the culture and the covert values of the tales. The aim was to compare and contrast tales from around the world and look at their similarities and differences so as to understand how they represent everyday life.

Stage 6: Release of the book and contact with the local community

The project is at the stage of distributing the books to the public library and the local schools, and the dissemination of the project. A blog in Catalan explains the experience and provides access to some bilingual material to anyone interested. Participants and volunteers, helped by educators, also produced a video presenting the project in different languages. See: www.youtube.com/watch?v=nmhQLb_wNc8&feature=player_embedded.

A formal presentation was arranged to explain the project and its results. Local schools, families and educators were invited to hear some participants explain the positive experience of creating a multilingual environment and their feelings of confidence in their role as educators now that the book has been published.

The main results of the project

To assess the results of the project after the first years of its implementation, research was conducted parallel to its development. Data collection used a mixed-method approach including ethnographic registers, in-depth interviews, sociolinguistic questionnaires and language proficiency tests. Only a summary of the main results can be presented here, but for a full account see Oller and Vila (2011) and Oller (in press).

The benefits of the project were individual, social and communitarian. The women's proficiency in writing in Catalan increased dramatically, much to their individual benefit. They reported a dramatic enhancement of their support for their children's homework, and of their ability to understand and communicate with teachers or others in their everyday lives. Social networks were created among the participants and the local volunteers.

And immigrant mothers became far more aware of the value of maintaining their L1 and cultural traditions, empowering the family literacy practices in their L1 as well as those activities promoted at school. The social and communitarian effects of the project were also considerable. The public library was transformed into a multilingual space. The attendance of immigrant mothers in cultural places was normalized, books in the heritage languages of the local population were purchased and read, and new bilingual activities enhanced the recognition and use of different languages. All this provided a significant challenge to the prevailing prejudices in society and schools. Some teachers became interested in the bilingual book edited by the immigrant mothers whose children were in the teachers' classes.

Using bilingual materials as educational resources

Research has shown that dual language books have a positive effect on literacy achievement, motivation and family involvement in children's schooling (see Anderson *et al.*, 2010; Sneddon, 2009), yet immigrant students' languages are not taken into account in Catalan schools. In most 'multilingual' schools in Catalonia only the student population is multilingual, and, until now, their languages played no role in their education or in their daily school life. Therefore the potential of linguistic diversity for cultural enrichment is seldom realized.

Developing multilingual projects in Catalan schools

Catalan schools can use the bilingual storybook written by African mothers to start similar multilingual projects. Below are some suggestions:

- *Storytelling in different languages*. Invite families to share their fairy tales at school and to foster their knowledge of different languages and cultures. Oral storytelling can be developed in more than two languages if there are community volunteers or bilingual students who can be invited to help with translations. Other activities can include tasks such as providing multilingual labels for story characters and settings; constructing multilingual dictionaries, starting with the vocabulary used in the stories; and exploring different ways of beginning and ending a story in different cultures. Storytelling as a bilingual activity can be recorded and uploaded on to the school website.
- *Dramatization of fairy tales*. Students can role-play stories in various ways, using words based on the settings and characters of the book in different languages. For example, they can create their own puppets, draw pictures and produce animated videos or stage performances of

fairy tales. Parents can help with the design of the scenery and clothes, choose traditional music to accompany the performance, write dual language brochures or assess children's oral production in the L1.

- *Multilingual story translation and reading.* Teachers can introduce formal activities like reading and writing in various languages, preferably those of the community, but also international languages. Translation and reading activities can be developed as appropriate. Identity texts and traditional poems and songs are ideal materials for creating a class environment that celebrates language diversity.

- *Comparing stories and creating new multicultural texts.* Traditional stories can be contrasted and compared in terms of content. Hidden values and the symbolism of the tales and the characters can be analysed to explore different ways of transmitting cultural issues. The same tale may be found in several countries with variations in the plot. Children can explore the origin of tales, their hidden morals and purpose. Traditional tales can be adapted for children by incorporating characters, settings or values from other countries to overcome the supremacy of Western literature.

Activities of this kind can enhance children's knowledge of different traditions and cultures, and can also be an opportunity to involve immigrant families actively in school. The activities can be adapted to suit different ages and incorporated into various subject areas. All students can benefit, but especially newcomers who are learning a new language in school and cannot yet read or write in the L2 at their appropriate age level without the scaffolding provided by their first language.

Conclusion

The Interweaving Cultures Project tries to go beyond the traditional approach of monolingual print literacy to develop a multiliterate practice for creating a more inclusive society. Although our project is based on an adult activity in a public library, most of its ideas can be used in schools to foster multilingualism.

In Catalonia, and in Spain generally, more initiatives should promote the use of heritage languages in the curriculum or at least recognize them. The way in which literacy is understood in schools needs urgently to be changed to meet the challenges of a plural and modern society head-on. Schools have to fight against the prevailing cultural prejudices and stereotyping of immigrants. Introducing students' linguistic and cultural backgrounds in schools will help immigrant students to see their cultural heritage and identity valued in school while they learn the language and culture of the host society.

As Cummins (2001) has shown, the process of school adjustment and overall performance of immigrant students will benefit if the L1 plays a role in schooling. Although all students should certainly become proficient in the language of the school, the students' own languages also have a role to play. Multilingual schools offer exciting opportunities to draw on the linguistic resources of the community, even if few of the teachers speak the students' home languages. So using bilingual books created by the immigrant mothers of the students is a good way of acknowledging the value of cultural and linguistic diversity in schools. Featuring such resources in schools and public libraries can help to change the prevailing negative perception of African groups by the host society. Some of the bilingual books will be the first available in that community language and may draw the immigrants who speak the language into the normalized cultural spaces. Furthermore, local schools can raise awareness of the importance of maintaining and promoting the languages of the immigrant children to foster their academic performance and develop students' awareness of cultures about which they have little accurate information.

Linguistic diversity should be viewed as a resource with the potential to enrich the experience of schooling for all students, their parents and teachers. The bilingual book created by immigrant women in the Interweaving Cultures Project can be a good starting point for including immigrant students' first languages as educational materials in cultural spaces such as schools and public libraries.

Note
[1] This research was funded by a grant from the Government of Catalonia to encourage applied research on immigration (project reference: 2009ARF100017).

References
Actis, W. (2004) 'La escuela ante la diversidad sociocultural: Discursos de los principales agentes sociales referidos a las minorías étnicas de origen extranjero'. Paper presented at the Summer Course of Santiago de Compostela University, Spain. Online. www.colectivoioe.org/index.php/publicaciones_articulos/show/id/83 (accessed 2 June 2014).

Anderson, J., Anderson, A., Friedrich, N. and Kim, J.E. (2010) 'Taking stock of family literacy: Some contemporany perspectives'. *Journal of Early Childhood Literacy*, 10 (1), 33–53.

Baker, C. (1996) *Foundations of Bilingual Education and Bilingualism*. 2nd edn. Clevedon: Multilingual Matters.

Bronfenbrenner, U. (1979) *The Ecology of Human Development: Experiments by nature and design*. Harvard, MA: Harvard University Press.

Clarke, L.B., Sheridan, M.S. and Woods, E.K. (2010) 'Elements of healthy family–school relationships'. In Christenson, S.L. and Rechley, A.L. (eds) *Handbook of Family Partnerships*. London: Routledge, 61–79.

Colectivo Ioé (2007) *Inmigración, género y escuela: Exploración de los discursos del profesorado y del alumnado*. Madrid: CIDE-Ministerio de Educación y Ciencia. Online. www.colectivoioe.org/index.php/publicaciones_libros/show/id/59 (accessed 2 June 2014).

Cope, B. and Kalantzis, M. (eds) (2000) *Multiliteracies: Literacy learning and the design of social futures*. New York: Routledge.

Cummins, J. (2000) *Language, Power and Pedagogy: Bilingual children in the crossfire*. Clevedon: Multilingual Matters.

— (2001) *Negotiating Identities: Education for empowerment in a diverse society*. Los Angeles: California Association for Bilingual Education.

— (2006) 'Identity texts: The imaginative construction of self through multiliteracies pedagogy'. In Skutnabb-Kangas, T., Garcia, O. and Torres Guzman, M.E. (eds) *Imagining Multilingual Schools: Languages in education and glocalization*. Clevedon: Multilingual Matters, 51–68.

Desforges, C. and Abouchaar, A. (2003) *The Impact of Parental Involvement, Parental Support and Family Education on Pupil Achievements and Adjustment: A literature review* (Research Report RR433). London: Department for Education and Skills.

Gabrielli, L. (2010) *Los procesos de socialización de los hijos e hijas de familias senegalesas y gambianas en Cataluña*. Barcelona: Fundació Jaume Bofill.

González, N., Moll, L.C. and Amanti, K. (2005) *Funds of Knowledge: Theorizing practices in households and classrooms*. New Jersey: Lawrence Erlbaum Associates.

Gregory, E. and Williams, A. (2000) 'Work or play? Unofficial literacies in the lives of two East London communities'. In Martin-Jones, M. and Jones, K. (eds) *Multilingual Literacies: Reading and writing different worlds*. Amsterdam: John Benjamins, 37–69.

Gregory, E., Long, S. and Volk, D. (2004) 'A sociocultural approach to learning'. In Gregory, E., Long, S. and Volk, D. (eds) *Many Pathways to Literacy: Young children learning with siblings, grandparents, peers and communities*. London: Routledge, 6–20.

Heller, M. and Martin-Jones, M. (eds) (2001) *Voices of Authority: Education and linguistic difference*. Westport, CT: Ablex Publishers.

Lindholm-Leary, K. (2001) *Dual Language Education*. Clevedon: Multilingual Matters.

Martin-Jones, M. and Jones, K. (eds) (2000) *Multilingual Literacies: Reading and writing different worlds*. Amsterdam: John Benjamins.

Martin-Jones, M. and Saxena, M. (2003) 'Bilingual resources and "funds of knowledge" for teaching and learning in multiethnic classes in Britain'. *International Journal of Bilingual Education and Bilingualism*, 6 (3–4), 267–82.

OECD (2006) *Where Immigrant Students Succeed: A comparative review of performance and engagement in PISA 2003*. Paris: OECD.

Oller, J. (in press) 'Empowering immigrant women through bilingual fairy tales: Linking family and school literacy practices'. *Cultura y Educación*, 26 (3).

Oller, J. and Vila, I. (2011) 'Teixint Cultures: Un programa comunitario que promueve las distintas identidades culturales y construye un espacio público de diálogo y convivencia'. In García Castaño, F.J. and Kressova, N. (coord.) *Actas del I Congreso Internacional sobre Migraciones en Andalucía*. Granada: Instituto de Migraciones. Online. http://dialnet.unirioja.es/servlet/articulo?codigo=4051257 (accessed 2 June 2014).

Ortiz, M. (2008) 'Inmigración en las aulas: Percepciones prejuiciosas de los docentes'. *Papers Revista de Sociología*, 87, 253–68.

Schecter, S. and Cummins, J. (2003) *Multilingual Education in Practice: Using diversity as a resource*. Portsmouth, NH: Heinemann.

Sneddon, R. (2009) *Bilingual Books – Biliterate Children: Learning to read through dual language books*. Stoke-on-Trent: Trentham Books.

Street, B. (1984) *Literacy in Theory and Practice*. Cambridge: Cambridge University Press.

Taylor, L.K., Bernhard, J.K., Garg, S. and Cummins, J. (2008) 'Affirming plural belonging: Building on students' family-based cultural and linguistic capital through multiliteracies pedagogies'. *Journal of Early Childhood Literacy*, 8 (3), 269–94.

Thomas, W.P. and Collier, V. (1997) *School Effectiveness for Language Minority Students*. Washington, DC: National Clearinghouse for Bilingual Education.

Vélez-Ibáñez, C. and Greenberg, J. (1992) 'Formation and transformation of funds of knowledge among U.S. Mexican households'. *Anthropology and Education Quarterly*, 23 (4), 313–35.

Vila, I. and Casares, R. (2009) *Educación y sociedad: Una perspectiva sobre las relaciones entre la escuela y el entorno social*. Barcelona: Horsori.

Part Three

Multiliteracy pedagogy in practice

Children as authors

tongue rests with the ethnic minority communities themselves. We believe that English should be the medium of instruction in schools.

(Overington, 2012: 6)

The Department for Education is introducing a policy by which all children will learn a foreign language. While qualifications are currently available in a number of community languages (21 at GCSE and 25 at Asset), these qualifications will be downgraded and the impact on the teaching of these languages is likely to be very negative. This is the challenging context in which parents, concerned about their children's rapid loss of the home language as they become dominant in English upon starting school, struggle to maintain and develop the language. Teachers committed to the development of children's language skills also struggle to develop a multilingual pedagogy in an ever-changing curriculum environment.

Multilingual pedagogy in theory

Teachers have become more knowledgeable about the cognitive and educational benefits of bilingualism. They are more likely than in the recent past to encourage parents to use the first language at home, and to buy dual language books for the school library. However, these more positive attitudes are not readily translated into classroom practice: an understanding of how to develop an active multilingualism, or indeed how to use dual language books in the classroom, is less common.

The work of Cummins is particularly relevant to the context of the multilingual British classroom, and teachers who are trained and experienced in working with bilingual children are familiar with it. The concept of the Common Underlying Proficiency explains that cognitive skills transfer readily from one language to another and there is substantial research evidence that this applies to reading skills even where scripts are substantially different (Cummins, 1984; Cummins, 1991). Bialystok has explored further the complexity of this transfer of key reading skills and notes that a difference in script doubles the difficulty of transferring skills. The process of learning to read in two languages gives bilingual children 'a more complete understanding of the symbolic relationship between print and meaning than monolinguals' (Bialystok, 2004: 164). It is noticeable that both the Albanian and francophone children in the case studies described in this chapter are supported by the use of the Roman alphabet.

In particular, the children's awareness of many cognates between French and English lead them to play with the phonology and morphology of their two languages. While the concept of transfer of skills has been most commonly invoked to support the initial teaching of reading in the first language for children who speak a minority language, of particular relevance in the present study is the fact that the transfer of skills is bidirectional. Although the research strongly supports the benefits to bilingual children of education in both their languages (Cummins, 2000), this option is rarely available to speakers of minority languages in England. Cummins's framework for empowering minority students in such contexts (Cummins, 1986; Cummins, 2000) recommends the incorporation of pedagogical strategies to support and develop pupils' bilingualism as well as the building of partnerships with families and the wider community.

The importance of a first language to an individual's personal identity is recognized in Cummins's use of the term 'identity text' to describe books such as the one written by Magda, referred to above, produced in the classroom by bilingual pupils (Cummins and Early, 2011). By encouraging and supporting pupils to build on their language resources and their personal experiences, teachers validate their linguistic and cultural knowledge and develop self-esteem and pride in their language.

In addition to the transfer of literacy skills and the importance of language to personal identity, the pedagogical and cognitive implications of the process of translation by young children are directly relevant to the case studies described below. Young bilingual pupils' generally rapid development in English leads to them being commonly called upon to act as community interpreters. While this topic has been well documented (Valdes, 2003; Hall, 2004), there has been far less research into children as translators of written text. Harris developed the concept of natural translation and argues that it is a natural skill for bilinguals, a bidirectional cognitive competence limited only by their knowledge of their languages (Harris and Sherwood, 1978). Harris argues that because children who are bilingual are generally also bicultural, they pay much more attention to communicating meaning that is intelligible in a particular cultural context than to linguistic correctness in the target language (Harris, 1976). Malakoff and Hakuta have described translation as the 'metalinguistic skill par excellence' (1991: 146) and note that it 'provides an easy avenue to enhance linguistic awareness and pride in bilingualism' (163). Any translation requires decisions to be made as to whether to focus on 'adequacy' (remaining close to the source text) or 'acceptability' (closer to the norms of the target language) (Toury, 1980). While Harris's research suggests that children generally operate at the 'acceptability' end of the spectrum, it is interesting that the Albanian girls in the first case study, who are aware that dual language text requires the translator to remain close to the source text, are deliberately focusing on 'adequacy'.

New models of biliteracy are beginning to influence the development of pedagogies of bi- and multilingualism and multiliteracy. Garcia discusses different models in terms of the contexts of learning, the prevailing pedagogy and the desired outcomes of bilingual teaching. In the *convergent biliterate model*, she suggests that, when both languages are used for writing, the 'minority language practices are calqued on those of majority literacy practices' (Garcia, 2009: 342). While the writing of books in dual language format creates an expectation that the languages will be kept separate, the process of composing or translating using two languages brings into the classroom the practice of 'bilingual languaging' (Garcia, 2009: 342), the natural way in which bilinguals use their languages. This is much in evidence in the French case study below. A recent example of this, and of translanguaging practice, is to be found in the action research project that brought together teachers from mainstream primary and complementary schools in east London to develop and jointly deliver a multilingual pedagogy for their classrooms (Kenner and Ruby, 2012). The study offers examples of the linguistic and cognitive enrichment experienced by children studying similes in fairy tales in Bengali and English.

Developing the use of children's literature in multilingual classrooms

As schools in the UK became more diverse, one of the ways in which teachers worked to support children's languages and cultures was to seek literature that reflected these aspects of children's lives. Guidance was available to teachers on how to use children's literature to teach English to new learners of the language (Hester, 1981). Teachers looking for texts that reflected children's home languages as well as their personal experience worked creatively to meet children's needs through liaising closely with families and communities to develop story texts (Sneddon, 2009). They discovered that, through enquiring about children's home languages, they could build good relationships with families, which in turn offered them opportunities to make use of families' funds of knowledge in the classroom (Gonzalez *et al.*, 1993).

Bilingual book making in family workshops was pioneered in a very linguistically diverse school in east London by Clover and Gilbert who described 'using the rich language and cultural background of our families as a resource for the school' (1981: 6). They found that the books helped to develop good home–school links and to establish a true multicultural curriculum (Clover and Gilbert, 1981: 9). Inspired by Clover and Gilbert, in a school in which 20 languages were spoken, I ran a Mother and Child Writing Project to make bilingual books for the classroom on topics chosen by children and their mothers (Sneddon, 1986). While the two projects referred to above were primarily concerned with developing classroom multilingual pedagogy and home–school relationships, other literacy projects throughout the 1980s and 1990s extended the concept into creating professionally produced texts for a wider distribution. As demand for dual language books grew, commercial publishers responded. Mantra Lingua, at the time of writing the most widely known in the UK, publishes in 50 languages (Sneddon, 2009).

The recent availability of dual language books for young children in a wide range of languages prompted the Ethnic Minority Achievement Team in the east London borough of Redbridge to carry out an action research project. The Multilingual Resources for Children Project invited children and teachers to evaluate the books and develop new ways of using them in the classroom.

Pedagogy in practice: The school context

In 2006 a large supply of dual language books was made available to all primary schools in the Borough of Redbridge. The aim of the project (EMAT, 2007) was to create a reading culture that would support the development of literacy in children's home languages as well as in English (Sneddon, 2009). The teachers who developed this project were familiar with the work of Cummins and in particular with the concept of transfer of skills. This is strongly in evidence in the work of a Year 1 teacher in Christchurch School, a large primary school in which 80 per cent of children are bilingual and 30 different languages are spoken. The school was enthusiastic in its promotion of the project and the teacher developed a strategy to teach reading that made use of all children's languages. She used children's literature in dual language format to teach reading in English, choosing books that were available in the nine languages spoken at the time in her classroom. Parents were encouraged and supported to read to their children in both languages and to teach the children who wished to learn to read for themselves. This strategy enabled the teacher to monitor children's reading in all their languages, even though she could only herself read two of them, and supported the discussion of key texts of children's literature encountered multilingually.

Familiarity with Cummins's model of empowerment for minority students (Cummins, 1986) is also in evidence in the measures the school takes to promote the use of pupils' home languages. Children are encouraged to bring their friends to the lunchtime language clubs that are supported by parents and volunteers. Language knowledge and skills are shared and acknowledged publicly in assemblies, special cultural events and displays around the school. Multilingual activities are encouraged in the classroom and links are made with complementary schools that teach pupils' languages.

This is the context in which the children who feature in the two following case studies started on their journey to biliteracy. In a later interview Magda and Albana recall the significance of finding books in Albanian in the classroom and acknowledge the important role their teachers played in their biliteracy development (Sneddon, 2011a).

As well as learning to read with their mothers and producing books, they attended the Albanian lunch club, performed Albanian dances in school assembly and public events to celebrate refugee week, and were put in touch with Shpresa Programme, an Albanian complementary school. The francophone children also attended a lunchtime language club supported by their mothers.

Conducting the case studies

The first case study, of Magda and Albana, was initially part of a pilot study designed to explore the transferability of literacy skills across five different pairs of languages (Sneddon, 2009), as well as the impact of developing biliteracy on metalinguistic awareness and personal and learner identity. Four years later the researcher was invited by their teacher to observe the girls' development into becoming independent writers as well as the writing workshops organized for a group of francophone children, which feature in the second case study. For both groups, writing sessions were observed, audio-recorded and transcribed, and interviews were carried out with the children's mothers and their teachers. Whereas the study of the francophone children presents a snapshot in time as children are supported to compose and translate in their two languages, the study of the Albanian girls offers a longitudinal view of their development from readers into independent writers. Some time after their story was published, the girls were invited to comment together on the transcript of their discussions (Sneddon, 2012) and separately about their recollections of their journey to biliteracy (Sneddon, 2011a).

Magda and Albana reading and becoming authors

When I first encountered them, Magda and Albana were 6 years old and close to the end of their first year in primary school. They were born in

London of ethnic Albanian parents who had arrived in the UK as refugees in the early 1990s. The girls spoke only Albanian until they started nursery school, when both acquired English rapidly. When they joined their new class the teacher had arranged for them to have the additional support of an experienced teaching assistant who worked with a small group of bilingual pupils to ensure that they learned to read with understanding. When the teacher introduced dual language books in Albanian, both girls were keen to take them home. Both Magda and Albana's families were concerned that they were losing fluency in Albanian and both agreed to read regularly with their children in both languages.

By the time I met them and started recording Magda with her mother Miranda and Albana with Lere, the girls had been reading with their mothers for six months. From needing support with reading with understanding, they were now among the best readers in their class. The dual language books available to them were mostly folk tales widely known in Europe ('Red Riding Hood', 'Hansel and Gretel', 'Goldilocks') but also included modern stories from non-European cultures such as *The Swirling Hijab* (Robert, 2002) and *Handa's Hen* (Browne, 2002). While the books were chosen for the classroom to include the languages of all the children, they did not always reflect the children's cultures and there were no Albanian folk tales available.

As I observed them over a period of several months, just before and shortly after their summer holiday, the strategies used by the mothers to teach, and the girls to learn, become apparent. Magda always reads the Albanian text first. While she can read the English page fluently and with expression in English, she is intent on using what Miranda has taught her about the sound correspondence of Albanian letters and the phonic skills she has learnt in her English classroom to blend sounds in Albanian and decode the text:

> Magda: (reading title page) *Perçja valos …*
> Miranda: *Valez …*
> Magda: *valëzuese* (The swirling hijab). *Perçja e mamit tim është e zezë e butë dhe e ja, je*
> Miranda: (whispers) *gjerë*
> Miranda: Mmm.

> (Sneddon, 2009: 72)

Miranda corrects discreetly, avoiding interrupting the flow of Magda's reading.

While Albana reads with fluency and confidence, with Lere only correcting the position of the stress in longer words, at this stage neither girl is keen to discuss the story. On a second reading Magda and Miranda make meaning together, asking each other questions and then referring to the English text for confirmation:

> Miranda: *kotecit*, around, around hunted. Do you know English hunted?
> Magda: Yeah.
> Miranda: Can you explain?
> Magda: It's when, it's like you go somewhere and you look for, like when you go shopping ... and they were hunting, to look for Han ... Mondi.

The transcript of the observations reveals the full range of strategies that Magda and Albana have learned in their English class and that both are now deploying to make sense of the Albanian text. When Albana encounters the word *përvoje* (ordeal) which neither of them know in either language, Albana uses all the strategies she has learned in her English class: after reading both the English and the Albanian texts and scrutinizing the illustrations, she considers the context and what she knows of traditional stories. The text is a modern sequel to the story of Red Riding Hood. From her knowledge of the original tale she deduces the meaning of 'ordeal' in the context of Red Riding Hood's encounter with the wolf (Clynes and Daykin, 2003). Through a process of working across texts in both languages, multiple readings, asking questions and retelling the story, the girls developed into competent readers of simple children's stories.

The girls' skills were celebrated by the school and they were encouraged to start writing. With their mothers' help they started writing diaries in Albanian while they were both (separately) on holiday with grandparents in Albania. The girls are best friends; they mirror each other's behaviour. They agreed on a format for their diaries and also agreed on a format when it was suggested to them that they turn them into a narrative and make their own illustrated dual language books.

The quotation at the start of this chapter shows Magda reflecting at a later date on the process of becoming biliterate. Both girls note how proud they were when their personal stories were published by the school and borrowed by their friends from the school library. Albana recalls the response to her first book:

> Then I found out that lots of people liked it and I felt special. My teacher told the whole class and it was mentioned in assembly. And I felt really special because loads of people in my class and in my year group would come up and say, oh, look, I got your book and it's really good.

> (Sneddon, 2011a: 360)

At age 10, in their penultimate year in primary school, they approached their teacher about writing a dual language fiction book together. I was offered the opportunity to observe them over three sessions as they composed a narrative together in English and worked on it, section by section, to translate it into Albanian. Working together in a side room, they had no dictionaries or internet and worked entirely from their own resources.

As they compose their story the girls reveal just how, from their immersion in children's literature in primary school, they have learned to structure a narrative with multiple episodes, to build suspense, and to write realistic dialogue. Finding inspiration for the plot in the popular culture all around them, in films, television and video games, the girls tell a gripping story of the Computer Geek/*Geek Computri*, about an obsessive computer gamer called Jordan, who gets sucked into a virtual adventure inside his laptop and, after many twists of the plot, is rescued by his grandmother.

Magda and Albana at age 10 are proficient writers in English and this is the language they choose for their initial joint composition. As they start the process of translating, Albana explains the difficulties:

> in English it, like, makes sense. And then we try to translate it in Albanian, but it won't work. You have to try and find a word that's exactly like that but makes sense. Yes, you need to. ... In a sentence in English you say it, but in Albanian you swap all the words around.

As they work from their English text, Magda and Albana demonstrate a range of strategies: using windows of meaning of different sizes, sometimes trying to work word for word, then realizing 'we need to do the rest because it won't make sense'. They debate at length as they try to reflect a shade of meaning: '*nderkohë* – it's like meanwhile. But we were trying to find while. And we couldn't think of anything, so we just kept thinking'. Sometimes they work phrase by phrase, and may also find that a whole sentence can fall into place: 'just sometimes we just read like, I don't know, a whole, if it's like a small paragraph, we read it all and it just comes in your head, you just know it.' They discover the agony of trying to capture the word that is 'on the top of my nose'.

They also know that a dual language text requires a translation that remains very close to the original as both texts are presented in parallel on the page. In their first draft the girls found themselves unable to express 'at the side of his computer' in Albanian. They settle for *Kur ai pa nje dritë ne majt të kompjutrit* ('he saw a light on the left side of his computer') and Magda explains 'we're changing it to, like, left. Because we don't know.' To meet the requirement of translation in a dual language text, they then agreed to adjust the English text accordingly. When it comes to translating, the girls' skills in both languages are well balanced and they enjoy the challenge of creating an equivalent meaning for their English text, working together from their own resources.

Over the years that they have been working with dual language text, both reading and writing their own, the girls have greatly extended their vocabulary beyond the domestic sphere. Lere noted that 'she has learned words that I don't know' and it is noticeable that while working on the 'Computer Geek' story, these untutored translators have access, between them, to nearly all the vocabulary they need to tell a good story. While there are some spelling and grammatical errors, these are remarkably few given the very limited formal instruction the girls have received in Albanian.

The francophone children

The popularity of Magda and Albana's holiday stories led to the school identifying a group of francophone children and suggesting to their parents that they may like to work in small groups with their children to help them write dual language stories. The children were divided into two groups by age, and the present chapter focuses on the work of the younger group. The children in this group were aged from 4 to 6 and their families originated from the Democratic Republic of Congo, Cameroon, Morocco, Mauritius and France. While all the children used French in the home to varying degrees and several children had access to a third language (Bafon and Turkish), all had become dominant in English since they started school and none were ever heard to use their home language to each other in school. Like the Albanian mothers, the French-speaking ones were anxious about home language loss and were keen to support initiatives in the school to support its use.

A story was composed and translated over four sessions. A group of seven children met with a teacher and composed a text together over two sessions. While the children negotiated the general shape of the story, the types of characters and the dialogue, the teacher guided the structure, and the 'Dragon in the Jungle'/'*Le dragon dans la jungle*' emerged as a recognizable animal tale with repeated sequences of dialogue (Sneddon, 2011b). I recorded, as a participant observer, the second session during which the children translated their text with the help of two of their mothers, Pauline and Marianne.

Teachers and researchers have observed how reluctant bilingual children can be to use the language of the home in school, having noted what Cummins refers to as the 'invisible sign on the classroom wall that says English Only' (2007). The children were initially somewhat reluctant to use French in the school environment. Pauline engaged them in conversation in French about the story, then guided them through the translation process, offering first a whole English sentence to translate, then breaking it down to phrase and word level until she got a response from the children. Pauline, reading the first sentence to be translated:

> the tiger said please can you help stop the nasty dragon from destroying the jungle.
> Michelle: *la jungle.*
> Pauline: *comment on dit* the tiger said? How do you say tiger in French?
> Simone: *tigre.*
> Pauline: said?
> David: *a dit.*
> Pauline: *Bravo David! Le tigre a dit. Parfait! Comment on dit* please? (The tiger said. Perfect! How do you say please?)

As the children gained in confidence, so the windows of meaning got larger and they started offering whole phrases:

> Michelle: *le visage a le dragon* (the face of the dragon)

The children in this group are much younger than Magda and Albana and, while their vocabulary range is more limited, their knowledge of French is greater than is apparent at first. Whole phrases develop into short sentences:

> Pauline: what do you think you are doing?
> Emilie: *qu'est-ce que tu fais?* (what are you doing ?)

While the adults' aim for the activity is to produce two separate parallel texts, they are working with the children in a sophisticated way across languages as they negotiate the creation of equivalent meaning. As the children struggle to find words, they start experimenting with language boundaries within words, exploring the sound of cognates, trying out *tigèr*, pronounced as a French word and as *TIGRRRRRE!* for *tigre*; *parrète* for *perroquet* (parrot); *tronque* for *trompe* (trunk) and the hybrid li-*on*, pronounced half in English and half in French. The word identically spelt jungle/*jungle* is modulated as a continuum between the two languages.

The children's cross-language work demonstrates their understanding of the morphology of their languages as they try out *trické le dragon* for tricked the dragon and *détroy* for destroy.

A group of older children, aged 7 to 10, developed a very complex and scary story entitled 'The Giant Evil Teddy Bear and the Crystal Ball'/ '*L'Enorme Nounours Malveillant et la Boule de Cristal*', using all the advice they had been given in English lessons to use rich and varied vocabulary, resulting in a serious translation challenge, not only to themselves, but also to the mothers assisting them.

All three dual language books, the two French and the Albanian, were illustrated by the children, with the older children designing the whole book, and were accompanied by recordings on CD of the text in both languages. They were presented at a book launch in school with refreshments, invited guests and readings by the authors.

Multilingual pedagogies in the classroom
Magda:

> I never imagined that I would actually make a book, and, reading all those English and Albanian books, and now when I think, when I read an English book, I'm always, like, 'I've made a book as well'.

> (Sneddon, 2011a: 360)

Teachers committed to empowering the bilingual pupils in their very linguistically diverse schools have proven to be creative in facing the challenges presented by an educational policy that is highly ambivalent about bilingualism and resolutely monolingual and monocultural in its curriculum. The tradition in the UK of using children's literature in dual language format as a starting point to develop multiliteracy skills and engage with minority linguistic communities goes back to the 1970s. New generations of teachers are discovering the value of children's literature, and book making in particular, to draw out the links between language, story and personal identity. Since the 1970s the technology available has greatly improved the scope, design and dissemination of children's work. As children and teachers in multilingual urban settings have explored new technology they have created multimedia and multimodal, as well as multilingual, texts and made them available as resources to a much wider audience through the internet (Lotherington, 2011).

What teachers involved in book making are also rediscovering is the confidence that children gain from finding their language recognized and valued in school. The young children creating the Dragon story are greatly enjoying playing with words and sounds across their languages. The excitement of meeting the cognitive challenge of writing in their less familiar language is much in evidence in the work of Magda and Albana over time, as is their pride in becoming authors.

The process of book-making is highly motivating for children and it offers a model of writing development that can be readily adapted to most multilingual school environments, even in a very monolingualizing context. In many of its interpretations since the 1970s it has involved families and the wider community as partners in biliteracy development. However, while it begins to bring the languages of the community into the classroom, a great deal more could be done in classrooms to make use of bilingual children's language and cultural knowledge and skills. The practices described above are still very much based on English classroom practices. Dual language books are primarily a school-based form of literacy and their use is not uncontroversial; they privilege English and encourage a traditional language teaching model that keeps languages separate. There are interesting creative challenges in exploring ways in which children can bring together more holistically the world of home and school (the 'interconnected worlds' of Kenner and Ruby, 2012), not just through using children's personal knowledge and experience, but also in making use of more authentic literacy materials and in building more directly on the natural multilingual practices of bilinguals. The kinds of discussions that Magda and Albana have about expressing shades of meaning in translation and the ways in which the francophone children explore the structure of words in their two languages indicate how making use of children's translanguaging skills, their intuitive metalinguistic understanding and their bidirectional cognitive competence might further their learning. There is much exploration to do in English schools to develop a multilingual pedagogical model and to extend it beyond working with literature, with story, to use translanguaging for learning across the curriculum, as Kenner and Ruby (2012) have shown in their work.

Note

[1] The author would like to thank all children, parents and teachers whose willing participation made the research possible. 'The Computer Geek' is online at www. uel.ac.uk/duallanguagebooks/young_authors.htm.

References

Anderson, J. (2008) 'Initial teacher education for teachers of Arabic, Mandarin Chinese, Panjabi and Urdu'. In Kenner, C. and Hickey, T. (eds) *Multilingual Europe: Diversity and learning*. Stoke-on-Trent: Trentham Books, 152–7.

Anderson, J., Gregory, E. and Kenner, C. (2008) 'The National Languages Strategy in the UK: Are minority languages still on the margins?' In Helot, C. and de Mejia, A.M. (eds) *Integrated Perspectives towards Bilingual Education: Bridging the gap between prestigious bilingualism and the bilingualism of minorities*. Clevedon: Multilingual Matters, 183–202.

Baetens Beardsmore, H. (2003) 'Who is afraid of bilingualism?'. In Dewaele, J.M., Housen, A. and Wei, L. (eds) *Bilingualism: Beyond basic principles*. Clevedon: Multilingual Matters, 10–27.

Bialystok, E. (2004) 'The impact of bilingualism on language and literacy development'. In Bhatia, T.K. and Ritchie, W.C. (eds) *The Handbook of Bilingualism*. Oxford: Blackwell, 577–602.

Bourne, J. (1989) *Moving into the Mainstream: EAL provision for bilingual pupils*. Windsor: NFER-Nelson.

Browne, E. (2002) *Handa's Hen*. London: Mantra Lingua.

CILT – National Centre for Languages (2008) *Our Languages*. Online. www. ourlanguages.org (accessed 4 April 2013).

Clegg, J. (1996) 'Introduction'. In Clegg, J. (ed.) *Mainstreaming ESL: Case studies in integrating ESL students into the mainstream curriculum*. Clevedon: Multilingual Matters, 1–39.

Clover, J. and Gilbert, S. (1981) 'Parental involvement in the development of language'. *Multiethnic Educational Review*, 1 (3), 6–9.

Clynes, K. and Daykin, L. (2003) *Not Again Red Riding Hood*. London: Mantra Lingua.

Cummins, J. (1984) *Bilingualism and Special Education: Issues in assessment and pedagogy*. Clevedon: Multilingual Matters.

— (1986) 'Empowering minority students: A framework for intervention'. *Harvard Educational Review*, 56 (1), 18–36.

— (1991) 'Interdependence of first and second language proficiency in bilingual children'. In Bialystok, E. (ed.) *Language Processing in Bilingual Children*. Cambridge: Cambridge University Press, 70–89.

— (2000) *Language, Power and Pedagogy: Bilingual children in the crossfire*. Clevedon: Multilingual Matters.

— (2007) 'Evidence-based literacy strategies: Bilingualism as a resource within the classroom'. Paper presented at the *Bilingualism, Learning and Achievement* conference at London Metropolitan University, 3 March.

Cummins, J. and Early, M. (2011) *Identity Texts: The collaborative creation of power in multilingual schools*. Stoke-on-Trent: Trentham Books.

Department of Education and Science (1985) *Education for All*. London: Her Majesty's Stationery Office (HMSO).

Department for Education and Skills (2002) *Languages for All, Languages for Life*. Annesley: DfES.

EMAT (2007) *Developing Reading Skills through Home Languages Project*. London Borough of Redbridge: Ethnic Minority Advisory Team.

Eversley, J., Mehmedbegovic, D., Sanderson, A., Tinsley, T., von Ahn, M. and Wiggins, R.D. (2010) *Language Capital: Mapping the languages of London's schoolchildren*. London: Institute of Education and CILT.

Garcia, O. (2009) *Bilingual Education in the 21st Century: A global perspective*. Chichester: Wiley-Blackwell.

Gonzalez, N., Moll, Z., Floyd-Tenery, M., Rivera, A., Rendon, P., Gonzales, R. and Amanti, C. (1993) *Teacher Research on Funds of Knowledge: Learning from households*. Online. www.ncela.us/files/rcd/BE019122/EPR6_Teacher_Research_on_Funds.pdf (accessed 2 June 2014).

Hall, N. (2004) 'The child in the middle: Agency and diplomacy in language brokering events'. In Hansen, G., Malmkjaer, K. and Gile, D. (eds) *Claims, Changes and Challenges in Translation Studies*. Amsterdam: John Benjamins, 285–96.

Harris, B. (1976) *The Importance of Natural Translation* (Working Papers in Bilingualism, No. 12). Toronto: The Ontario Institute for Studies in Education.

Harris, B. and Sherwood, B. (1978) 'Translating as an innate skill'. In Gerver, D. and Sinaiko, W.H. (eds) *Language Interpretation and Communication* (Proceedings of the NATO Symposium on Language Interpretation and Communication, Giorgio Cini Foundation, Venice, 1977). Oxford: Plenum, 155–70.

Hester, H. (1981) *Stories in the Multicultural Primary Classroom: Supporting children's learning of English as an additional language*. London: Inner London Education Authority.

Kenner, C. and Ruby, M. (2012) *Interconnecting Worlds: Teacher partnerships for bilingual learning*. Stoke-on-Trent: Trentham Books.

Lotherington, H. (2011) *Pedagogy of Multiliteracies: Rewriting Goldilocks*. New York: Routledge.

Malakoff, M. and Hakuta, K. (1991) 'Translation skill and metalinguistic awareness in bilinguals'. In Bialystok, E. (ed.) *Language Processing in Bilingual Children*. Cambridge: Cambridge University Press, 141–66.

Overington, A. (2012) *A Brief Summary of Government Policy in Relation to EAL Learners*. Online. www.naldic.org.uk/Resources/NALDIC/Research%20and%20Information/Documents/Brief_summary_of_Government_policy_for_EAL_Learners.pdf (accessed 2 June 2014).

Rassool, N. (1997) 'Language policies for a multicultural Britain'. In Wodak, R. and Corson, D. (eds) *Language Policy and Political Issues in Education*. Vol. I of *Encyclopedia of Language and Education*. London: Kluwer Academic, 113–26.

Robert, N. (2002) *The Swirling Hijab*. London: Mantra Lingua.

Ruiz, R. (1984) 'Orientations in language planning'. *National Association for Bilingual Education Journal*, 8 (2), 15–34.

Sneddon, R. (1986) 'The mother and child writing group'. *Language Matters*, 2, 18–23.

— (2009) *Bilingual Books – Biliterate Children: Learning to read through dual language books*. Stoke-on-Trent: Trentham Books.

— (2010) 'Abetare and dancing: The story of a partnership'. In Lytra, V. and Martin, M. (eds) *Sites of Multilingualism: Complementary schools in Britain today*. Stoke-on-Trent: Trentham Books, 45–56.

— (2011a). 'Two languages – two voices: Magda and Albana become authors'. In Czerniawski, G. and Kidd, W. (eds) *The Student Voice Handbook: Bridging the academic/practitioner divide*. Bingley: Emerald, 351–64.

— (2011b) 'Le dragon dans la jungle/The dragon in the jungle'. *Race Equality Teaching*, 30 (1), 16–20.

— (2012) 'Telling the story of the Computer Geek: Children becoming authors and translators'. *Language and Education*, 1, 1–16.

Toury, G. (1980) *In Search of a Theory of Translation*. Tel Aviv: Porter Institute for Poetics and Semiotics.

Valdes, G. (2003) *Expanding Definitions of Giftedness: The case of young interpreters from immigrant communities*. Mahwah, NJ: Laurence Erlbaum.

Vertovec, S. (2007) *New Complexities of Cohesion in Britain: Super-diversity, transnationalism and civil-integration*. Wetherby: Communities and Local Government Publications.

Chapter 8

From a school task to community effort

Children as authors of multilingual picture books in an endangered language context

Anne Pitkänen-Huhta and Sari Pietikäinen

Introduction

Sari Pietikäinen

Figure 8.1: The Little Books

This chapter[1] tells the story of the journey of 'Little Books', multimodal and multilingual picture books created by a group of Sámi schoolchildren as a participatory literacy task in the context of endangered indigenous Sámi languages. The Sámi, who number approximately 60,000–80,000, are an indigenous people living in Scandinavia and north-west Russia. There are nine Sámi languages in all. The language with the highest number of speakers – around 30,000 – is Northern Sámi; others have as few as 250 to 400 speakers each (Aikio-Puoskari, 2005; Kulonen *et al.*, 2005). All Sámi languages are classified as endangered and there are no monolingual Sámi speakers left. As is the case for the children in this story, Sámi languages are part of the multilingual repertoire of their users.

These children speak Finnish and Northern Sámi and/or Inari Sámi and, to a varying degree, other languages. They are the youngest generation of Sámi speakers, the target of several language revitalization and maintenance activities, one of which is the mostly Sámi medium education in which they are taking part. In this context, the Little Books project is aimed at encouraging children to make use of their existing semiotic resources, indigenous languages included, and thus to value multilingualism in their everyday lives without losing sight of indigenous language revitalization. To facilitate this, we set a task which turned readers into authors and creators of their own learning materials – what we have termed 'participatory literacy'. By the term *participatory literacy*, we wish to connect the Little Books to Freirean pedagogy on the one hand, and to research on literacy practices (e.g. Street, 1984; Barton and Hamilton, 1998; Baynham and Prinsloo, 2009) on the other.

Pedagogically, we draw on the work of Freire (1970), who emphasized the importance of people's local and personal experiences as the starting points and materials for learning. Participatory pedagogy foregrounds the interaction between the learner and the broader society, and promotes the empowerment of learners, encouraging their awareness of their own capacity and their ability to create new knowledge and thereby make use of their knowledge in society (Auerbach, 1993; Auerbach, 1995; Ajayi, 2008). The institutional context of multilingualism, such as L2 or Content Language Integrated Learning (CLIL) classrooms, has traditionally relied on polarized binaries, boxing language into pairs of productive-receptive skills (i.e. reading–writing, speaking–listening), and dividing learners into L1 and L2 – native speakers and non-native speakers (Lotherington and Jenson, 2011: 233). These concepts are epistemologically grounded in the relative fixed views on social and linguistic worlds of speech communities and on flat literacies.

This chapter relates how we chose to step away from strict binaries and categorizations and tried to think out of the box. Rather than approaching languages as compartmentalized entities, we see languages as resources and language use as practices, although we do not lose sight of the role of the community and the use of networks in an endangered language context (Heller, 2011; Pietikäinen and Pitkänen-Huhta, 2013; Pennycook, 2010). The Little Books project was carried out against this backdrop, and was inspired by the work on multilingual educational materials in multilingual classrooms by Busch (Busch, 2006; Busch *et al.*, 2006; Busch and Busch, 2008). For the historical development of self-made materials, see our previous work on multimodality of multilingual experiences and practices (Pietikäinen *et al.*, 2008; Pietikäinen, 2012; Pitkänen-Huhta and Nikula, 2013), and also Schreger and Pernes (Chapter 9, this volume).

The project[2] lasted for one school year and involved four steps: raising multilingual awareness; making the books; printing the books in the chosen languages; and launching the books.

The school where the project was carried out is a relatively small multilingual primary school of about one hundred pupils in Finnish Sámiland in the northernmost part of Finland. The languages used as the medium of education in this school include Finnish, Northern Sámi and Inari Sámi. The three Sámi languages spoken in Finland – Northern Sámi, Inari Sámi and Skolt Sámi – and Swedish and English are taught as a second, national or foreign language. All the pupils speak Finnish fluently and approximately 70 per cent of them take part in Sámi education: about half of them in Sámi medium education and the rest learning Sámi as a second language. The two Sámi groups involved in the Little Books project are in joint classrooms where pupils at different grades learn together with the same teacher, as is typical of small schools in rural communities like this one. The two classrooms we worked with have pupils from preschool to the 3rd Grade (i.e. 6–10 years old) and from the 3rd to the 6th Grade (i.e. 10–12 years old). All the children are multilingual, using Finnish and at least one of the Sámi languages in their daily lives, with many using other languages too, generally English or other Sámi languages. The language policy favours using Sámi language only for the activities, but in practice the children communicate in Finnish with each other, and with the children from the Finnish classrooms. And as there is still a dearth of Sámi teaching and learning materials, many of the resources are in Finnish.

Below, in four episodes, we tell the story of the steps involved in making and circulating the Little Books. The analysis is based on multimodal ethnographic and discursive data and each episode starts with pictures and vignettes illustrating the activity under focus.

Episode 1: Raising multilingual awareness

Sari Pietikäinen

Figure 8.2: Anna-Mari's visualization of multilingual repertoire

Children sit in the classroom together with the teacher and the researcher, colouring the picture of the human figure they were given. They visualize their multilingual repertoire by colouring different parts of the figure to represent different languages. Some add new elements (flowers, flags, a crown, a face) to the figure, some move about in the classroom to look at what others are doing. In the end, we form a circle and children take turns at showing their drawings to others. We talk about the languages shown on the figures, what colours have been chosen and where on the figure they are placed.

The guiding principle for the whole project was that change in language practices depends on first raising awareness. Our goals, set out together with the teachers and based on the previous discourse-ethnographic work in this school and the surrounding Sámi community (Pietikäinen *et al.*, 2008; Pietikäinen and Pitkänen-Huhta, 2013), were to valorize multilingual resources at the school and, importantly, to support enhancing the value and use of indigenous languages among the children. Sometimes, in endangered language contexts, multilingualism can be seen as a threat. However, in this project we start with the fact that indigenous Sámi languages are part of the children's multilingual repertoires, and should be seen as one resource among others. The role and status of different languages in one's repertoire can change during one's life and the competences in, and intensity of use, varies accordingly. Even partial competence is valuable and can be utilized in meaningful practices.

We aimed at creating opportunities for the children to engage in personally meaningful activities and practices and thereby find a space for their active participation (Norton and Toohey, 2001: 310; Watson-Gegeo, 2004). Language practices are an inherent part of certain social, historical, cultural and political contexts and learners' personal trajectories and previous experiences are central in the appropriation and transformation of practices. In addition, printed materials in Sámi languages are scarce. Consequently we tried to find ways to develop multilingual Sámi learning materials and practices together with the teachers and pupils. And since literacy skills are highly valued in education in general, we wished the children to engage in such activities in the endangered language.

We started awareness raising with a group discussion with members of each class – pupils, teacher and researchers on site – about the languages they hear, speak, see and read in their daily lives and with whom they use them. We discussed the different ways of talking and using languages so as to encourage the children to take note of the various ways in which languages are used. The questions aimed to encourage the children to reflect on the multilingualism around them and on the position of Sámi languages in this environment.

As a way to gather information about the children and their perception of their linguistic repertoires, we asked each child to fill in a two-page questionnaire about their background, language networks and language attitudes. The questionnaire shed light on the wide range of multilingualism present in the two classrooms: these 17 children between them used 13 different languages and 7 imaginary languages (see below). After filling in the questionnaires and talking about language repertoires, our next activity concerned visualizing one's multilingual repertoires in a drawing task. The children were given a sheet of white paper (A4) showing the outline of a human figure[3] with its left hand raised in greeting, and plenty of crayons for colouring. The children were asked to think about a language, attribute a colour to it, and then colour the language on a chosen part of the human figure. The children set to work immediately and enthusiastically – clearly drawing is a familiar classroom activity. When everyone had finished their colouring, they each showed their drawing and talked about the languages they had chosen to display on the figure, where they had placed them, and why. The discussion was video- and audiotaped.

The children seemed to be happy to talk about their languages and their choices of colours and where they had placed them. Their accounts and drawings highlighted the multiplicity of language resources around them. While some of the languages mentioned – such as Sámi languages, Finnish and English – were closely tied in with their everyday practices, others – such as Serbian, German and Danish – were souvenirs from summer holidays, or related to desires or future aspirations – such as Chinese. This activity also encouraged a flexible, creative approach by some children towards the boundaries and categories related to languages. It was intriguing to see how 9-year-old Anna-Mari explains 2 of the 11 languages she mentioned within her repertoire:

Extract 1[4]

Anna-Mari	(shows the drawing to everyone and points to one specific point in the drawing)
	Koirakieli on tässä koska mie ymmärrän koirakieltä niiden silmistä ja luonteesta.
	[Dog language is here because I understand dog language from their eyes and character.]
Researcher	*Onko sulla esimerkkiä siitä koirakielestä kun sä itse puhut sitä?*
	[Do you have an example of that dog language when you talk it yourself?]
Anna-Mari	*No mie haukun ja vingun ja kaikkea mitä mie osaan koirakieltä.*
	[Well I bark and whine and all that I can in dog language.]
Girl	*Sitten se ulvoo.*
	[Then she howls.]
Anna-Mari	*Ulvon kotona. siansaksa on täällä ylhäällä koska se on kaikkein helpoin kieli.*
	[I howl at home. Pig Latin is up here because that's the easiest language of all.]

Anna-Mari's experience of the value and function of dog language and gibberish language gives us a glimpse of her creative take on language resources. Children have probably always used imaginary languages. It is common to play with language so as to have fun, exclude others or to strengthen bonding of the group (see e.g. Byrd and Mintz, 2010). Anna-Mari does not want to limit her repertoire only to languages taught at school and her idea of language does not follow fixed linguistic classifications. Her account illustrates her creativity and invention as a resource for participation. Her choices follow neither the default norms of the school or community, nor the normative views of multilingualism in educational institutions.

Episode 2: Designing the book

Sari Pietikäinen

Figure 8.3: The Sámi version of the book by Merja

Children sit quietly in class and work on the books with concentration. Some have difficulty deciding on the topic and the teacher helps them. All are eager to become authors for the first time and all wish to finish the task on time. The whole task appears to be a truly joint effort for the classroom.

This step of the task was intended to encourage children to make use of their existing resources and thereby to show them that even limited linguistic resources can be used in creating meaningful literacy practices. Writing is not always a task that pupils engage in eagerly: younger children with limited language skills may find writing a difficult and strenuous task or consider writing in the classroom not to be very 'cool'. In these classrooms, too, some of the pupils seemed reluctant to engage in writing. It appeared that writing is often associated with practising the standard variant or drilling language structures and, particularly with Sámi, writing was experienced as difficult and even boring. So we wanted to evoke a positive, 'cool' mood around this activity and marketed it to the students as a real-world task in which they would become authors for the first time: they would create a book that would be printed showing the name and picture of the author; there would be a book launch and the book would be circulated beyond the classroom.

Designing a book represented an important and recognized practice for the community. Literacy, that is written and printed text in this case, represents permanence, stability and transferability of knowledge and is therefore valued by indigenous communities (Pietikäinen and Pitkänen-Huhta, 2014). For language users and learners, this task provided an opportunity to put their – sometimes limited – skills to use in a way that would benefit the whole community and its practices. Accordingly the process of learning an indigenous language became even more meaningful for the children. To ensure their engagement in the task, it was important that the task was multimodal and involved both written text and drawing, as the pupils' literacy skills varied considerably across an age range of six years. Drawing is a familiar school task for children of this age and so its inclusion appeared natural. The children were encouraged to use whatever resources they had available: some were good at writing stories and some were good at visualizing. The multimodality of the task gave the children alternative ways of expressing themselves (Busch and Busch, 2008; Krumm, 2001; Pietikäinen *et al.*, 2008; Pietikäinen, 2012; Nikula and Pitkänen-Huhta, 2008).

Along with the crayons, the pupils were given empty frames for the book, all containing five openings with two lines on the left-hand side indicating a space for the verbal story and an empty page on the right for the drawing. It was agreed that they would write the story in the Sámi language of the classroom: Northern Sámi or Inari Sámi. Designing the book took two months, with the children working on it in their Sámi language classes and also their art classes. The teachers reported that the children worked eagerly and enthusiastically on the task throughout the two months, so it was clear that they found the task interesting and meaningful.

The pupils were given a free hand in deciding what kind of book they wished to design. The topics of the books were not predetermined and indeed the children chose very different kinds of topics, with different kinds of justifications and backgrounds. Many topics seemed to arise from children's personal experiences. Petteri built the story around a specific kind of stick he wished to have: *no mailasta kun minä en saanu koskaan oikeanlaista mailaa* [well about the stick because I never got the right kind of stick]. Merja wrote about a miraculous night when she had a remarkable dream: *no ku minä nukuin sellasen ihmeellistä unta* [well because I slept and had a miraculous dream]. Some just invented a story. Aslak wrote about a cat and a dog: *noo (.) nnn no minä keksin sen* [well hmm well I made it up]. But his choice was also related to his personal wish to have a cat or a dog that was prevented by his little brother's allergy to animals (*ku minun isä on allerginen niille ja minun pikkuveli myös – niinku kerran joku koira nuoli minun pikkuveli Mattia kun minun isä veti sitä pulkassa ja Matti vaan nauroi mutta sitten sen naama vaan alko punottaa* ['cause my father is allergic to them and my little brother too – like once when a dog licked my little brother Matti when my father dragged him in a sledge and Matti just laughed but then his face turned red]). Some children were recycling familiar story genres, as Xia did: *se kertoo Viljamin mummosta joka on joskus ollu vanha kummitus* [it tells about Viljami's granny who has once been an old ghost].

The next stretch of interaction illustrates participatory literacy in practice, where the learners are truly involved and take up peer teaching roles in jointly constructing the story and thus support each other's language learning. The extract is from a conversation at the end of the discussion when the pupils presented their books to each other. Riina wanted to translate her story to the researcher and began to tell her story, which she wrote in Inari Sámi, in Finnish. She is helped by Merja and Aslak:

Extract 2

Riina	*Olipa kerran (.) tyttö (.) se* [Once upon time there was a girl she]
Merja	*se kasvatti* [she grew]
Riina	*se halusi (.)* [she wanted to]
Merja	(Sámi) *synnyttää* [create]
Riina	*-nnyttää (.) kukan (.) sitten tyttö huo-huomasi (.) kukan (.) sitten (.) tyttö (.) mietti (.) että (.) mitä jos (.) olisi (.) viidakko (.) ja (.) olisi (.) myös (.) lintu* [create a flower then the girl no-noticed a flower then the girl thought that what if there was a jungle and there was also a bird]
....	
Riina	*ja (.) minä (.) voi-sin..mennä (.) uimaan hui* (unclear)

	[and I could go swimming]
Researcher	(laughs)
Riina	*hiu (.) ääk (.) Chirri (.) mitä (.) Aslak (.) mikä on (a Sámi word) suomeksi*
	[oh Chirri what Aslak what is (a Sámi word) in Finnish]
Aslak	*ihmettä*
	[[what] on earth]
Riina	*mitä ihmettä (.) Chirrii (.) no jaa (.) ei se haittaa*
	[what on earth Chirrii well aha it doesn't matter]
Researcher	(laughs)
Merja	*Chirri on minun koira*
	[Chirri is my dog]

This conversation shows how Riina starts the story and Merja twice offers her the right verbs. Later Riina asks Aslak for help with a Sámi word and Aslak helps her. This piece of interaction shows how this project was not only about the final product – their written material – but also about providing opportunities for student collaboration and shared knowledge building and learning, thus strengthening participatory pedagogical practices.

Episode 3: Choosing the languages

Sari Pietikäinen

Figure 8.4: The Inari Sámi storyline (The komondor was washing itself. A basset hound was with it.) with translations into Northern Sámi, Swedish and English

Children sit in the classroom together with the teachers and the researcher and talk about the books and the languages they wish to choose for the story to be translated into. When the books are finished, each child author is photographed, so that a picture of the author appears on the back cover of the book. After the activity is finished in the school, it spreads into the

Sámi community and into the research community, as the teachers and the researcher search for translators.

In this stage of the activity, we could see language policies in action. Children's and teachers' negotiations about which languages to include and the children's explanations concerning their choices encapsulated the local language policy. To encourage children to recognize and reflect further on their multilingual resources, they were again given a free hand to determine which languages they wished to include in their books in addition to the two Sámi languages spoken in the classrooms. The policy decision to include the two Sámi languages had been made jointly with the teachers at the outset and reflects partly the institutional conditions and partly the emerging practice of the teachers to use both Northern Sámi and Inari Sámi when talking to the pupils. The linguistic closeness of these two languages makes this relatively easy. This situated negotiation of language policy is an instance of official and unofficial language policies becoming the practice in a local situation.

Within this local situation, the children were free to choose the languages into which they wished their stories to be translated. In the following extract, we see the teachers, researcher and children talking about the possible languages in translations:

Extract 3

Researcher	*Ehotelkaa vaan (.) se on teiän kirja.*
	[Just make suggestions it's your book.]
Petteri	*Kaikki saamen kielet.*
	[All Sámi languages.]
Researcher	*Se on hurjan hieno ajatus.*
	[That's a really great idea.]
Lasse	*Japani*
	[Japanese]
	(laughter)
Researcher	(laughs)
Lasse	*Kiina se oli.*
	[It was Chinese.]

At the beginning of Extract 3, the researcher prompts the pupils to suggest languages for the translations. Petteri's quick response to the researcher's prompt suggests his awareness of the response expected: the school is expected to promote Sámi languages in all situations. Petteri wishes to adhere to this, perhaps to show that he is a good student and knows what is appropriate. Lasse's response to include Japanese or Chinese, however, suggests that he wants to set himself apart from the official language policy and include something exotic and unexpected.

Invented languages are included in the languages into which the children can choose to have their stories translated. Saarakaisa suggests that Pig Latin and I-language (an invented language where all vowels are replaced by the letter *i*) should be included (*siansaksaksi (.) i-kielellä* [Pig Latin ... I-language]) in translations and later she adds Kontti-language. Saarakaisa's suggestion of mixed languages is interesting: *tai sitte semmosia jossa ois sekakieliä* [or then such where there would be mixed languages].

Literacy practices are deeply networked (see Barton and Hamilton, 1998) and often a community effort, especially when vernacular literacies are involved (Jones *et al.*, 2001). Here too, the community was involved in the process of translating the little stories, and the participants used their networks to find people who were able to do this. When the decision was made in class about the languages to be included in the book, the teachers and the researcher set out to find translators. The teachers did the Northern Sámi and Inari Sámi translations as standard written versions, and found a translator in the community to do Skolt Sámi. To respond to Petteri's request to have his text translated into as many Sámi languages as possible, we found translators for Kildin Sámi and Umeå Sámi through our research network. Translations into various other languages (including Swedish, Russian, Spanish, French and Norwegian) were made by team members or our colleagues at the Department of Languages at the University of Jyväskylä. The translation into Chinese was done by a daughter-in-law of one of the team members. Thus community effort and crowdsourcing were very apparent.

Episode 4: Launching the books

Sari Pietikäinen
Figure 8.5: The launch party

At the book launch party, the children came up one by one to receive their copies of the book, and then joined a happily chatting group of children who were eating snacks, drinking lemonade and comparing their books.

Special attention was paid to the materiality of the books. It was a central element in turning the school activity into the physical presence and concomitant status of a published book, thus valuing the vernacular mundane practices. The printing process entailed several steps. After the translations came in, the original books were taken to a printing house where the books were printed on thick cardboard to make them look and feel like real books. All the translations with their various orthographies were typeset and the photograph of the author placed on the back cover.

Once the books were printed they were circulated to their readers within and outside the school. A book launch party was held in the classrooms and each author was given author copies of the book. Invitations to the launch were also sent to the local media. The children and the researcher were interviewed by local journalists on the radio and Sámi television news. Copies of the books were also given to the teaching materials section of the Sámi Parliament and a few months later more books were printed so that the Parliament could send a set of copies of these books to every Sámi classroom in Finland.

The move from the institutional space of the school into the spaces of the children's homes, the local media and the Sámi political space gave the books their ultimate legitimation as 'real' books and to the children as 'real' authors. The journey of these Little Books from the classroom into the public domain transformed the school task into a community effort with a potentially big impact.

Conclusion

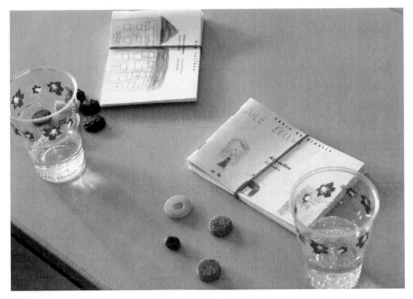

Sari Pietikäinen

Figure 8.6: Little Books ready for circulation

These books present a small-scale model of participatory literacy. In this model, the organizing principle was to provide such practices in spaces that invite and strengthen children's participation. In this project, this was achieved by giving children the freedom to make use of their multilingual repertoires as they saw fit in that situation, while at the same time respecting the institutional conditions and practices. Equally crucially, multimodality was given a central role. Also important to the model was that the materiality of the books was taken seriously to produce a permanent outcome from otherwise unrecognized and developing practice. Furthermore this facilitated the circulation of the participatory practice beyond the classroom. A final element of the model was the making of the books as a community effort. With these elements combined in the model, we aimed at bypassing fixed views of language, competence, proficiency and skills, and instead provided space for creating literacy practices that are meaningful for both the individuals and the community.

Notes

[1] This chapter is produced within the context of a research project called Peripheral Multilingualism (www.peripheralmultilingualism.fi) funded by the Academy of Finland.

[2] We have changed the names of the children, even though as the authors of these books the children may be recognizable via their connections to the place, the books and so on. We also want to acknowledge the help and support of Brigitta Bush and Leena Huss in designing and carrying out this project.

[3] We wish to thank Brigitta Busch for sharing with us this figure and practices around it. For use of this and similar kinds of figures in other multilingual contexts, see Busch *et al.* (2006); Busch and Busch (2008); Krumm (2001).

[4] The transcription conventions are (.) = pause, (word) = transcriber's comments, [word] = English translation.

References

Aikio-Puoskari, U. (2005) 'The education of the Sámi in the comprehensive schooling of three Nordic countries: Norway, Finland and Sweden'. *Gáldu čála – Journal of Indigenous Peoples Rights*, 2, 5–34.

Ajayi, L. (2008) 'Meaning-making, multimodal representation, and transformative pedagogy: An exploration of meaning construction instructional practices in an ESL high school classroom'. *Journal of Language, Identity and Education*, 7 (3–4), 206–29.

Auerbach, E. (1993) 'Re-examining English only in the ESL classroom'. *TESOL Quarterly*, 27 (1), 9–32.

— (1995) 'The politics of ESL classroom: Issues of power in pedagogical choices'. In Tollefson, J.W. (ed.) *Power and Inequality in Language Education*. New York: Cambridge University Press, 9–33.

Barton, D. and Hamilton, M. (1998) *Local Literacies: Reading and writing in one community*. London: Routledge.

Baynham, M. and Prinsloo, M. (eds) (2009) *The Future of Literacy Studies*. Basingstoke: Palgrave Macmillan.

Busch, B. (2006) 'Material development for linguistic diversity and intercultural learning'. In Alexandre, N. and Busch, B. (eds) *Literacy and Linguistic Diversity in a Global Perspective: An intercultural exchange with African countries*. Graz: European Centre for Modern Languages, Council of Europe Publishing, 75–90.

Busch, B. and Busch, T. (2008) *Von Menschen, Orten und Sprachen: Multilingual leben in Österreich*. Klagenfurth and Celovec: Drava.

Busch, B., Jardine, A. and Tjoutuku, A. (2006) *Language Biographies for Multilingual Learning* (PRAESA – Occasional Papers No. 24). Online. www.praesa.org.za/files/2012/07/Paper24.pdf (accessed 3 June 2014).

Byrd, D. and Mintz, T.H. (2010) *Discovering Speech, Words, and Mind*. Chichester: Wiley-Blackwell.

Freire, P. (1970) *Pedagogy of the Oppressed*. New York: Continuum.

Heller, M. (2011) *Paths to Post-Nationalism: A Critical ethnography of language and identity*. Oxford: Oxford University Press.

Jones, K., Martin-Jones, M. and Bhatt, A. (2001) 'Languages and literacies for autonomy'. In Martin-Jones, M. and Jones, K. (eds) *Multilingual Literacies: Reading and writing different worlds*. Amsterdam: John Benjamins, 319–52.

Krumm, H.J. (2001) *Kinder und ihre Sprachen – lebendige Mehrsprachigkeit*. Vienna: Eviva.

Kulonen, U.-M., Seurujärvi-Kari, I. and Pulkkinen, R. (eds) (2005) *The Sámi: A cultural encyclopaedia*. Helsinki: Suomalaisen Kirjallisuuden Seura.

Lotherington, H. and Jenson, J. (2011) 'Teaching multimodal and digital literacy in L2 settings: New literacies, new basics, new pedagogies'. *Annual Review of Applied Linguistics*, 31, 226–46.

Nikula, T. and Pitkänen-Huhta, A. (2008) 'Using photographs to access stories of learning English'. In Kalaja, P., Menezes, V. and Ferreira Barcelos, A.M. (eds) *Narratives of Learning and Teaching EFL*. Basingstoke: Palgrave, 171–85.

Norton, B. and Toohey, K. (2001) 'Changing perspectives on new language learners'. *TESOL Quarterly*, 35 (2), 307–22.

Pennycook, A. (2010) *Language as a Local Practice*. London: Routledge.

Pietikäinen, S. (2012) 'Experiences and expressions of multilingualism: Visual ethnography and discourse analysis in research with Sámi children'. In Martin-Jones, M. and Gardner, S. (eds) *Multilingualism, Discourse and Ethnography*. London: Routledge, 163–78.

Pietikäinen, S. and Pitkänen-Huhta, A. (2013) 'Multimodal literacy practices in the indigenous Sámi classroom: Children navigating in a complex multilingual setting'. *Journal of Language, Identity & Education*, 12 (4), 230–47.

— (2014) 'Dynamic multimodal language practices in multilingual indigenous Sámi classrooms in Finland'. In Gorter, D., Zenotz, V. and Cenoz, J. (eds) *Minority Languages and Multilingual Education: Bridging the local and the global*. Heidelberg: Springer, 137–57.

Pitkänen-Huhta, A. and Nikula, T (2013) 'Teenagers making sense of their foreign language practices: Individual accounts indexing social discourses'. In Benson, P. and Cooker, L. (eds) *The Applied Linguistic Individual: Sociocultural approaches to autonomy, agency and identity*. Sheffield: Equinox, 104–18.

Pietikäinen, S., Alanen, R., Dufva, H., Kalaja, P., Leppänen, S. and Pitkänen-Huhta, A. (2008) 'Languaging in Ultima Thule: Multilingualism in the life of a Sámi boy'. *International Journal of Multilingualism*, 5 (2), 77–89.

Street, B. (1984) *Literacy in Theory and Practice*. Cambridge: Cambridge University Press.

Watson-Gegeo, K.A. (2004) 'Mind, language, and epistemology: Toward a language socialization paradigm for SLA'. *The Modern Language Journal*, 88 (3), 331–50.

Chapter 9

The big world of 'Little Books'

Christian Schreger and Stefan Pernes

Introduction

The idea of making books with children is not new. As part of his struggle against the imposition of official government reading primers in France, Célestin Freinet (1896–1966) elevated book making to cult status within the 'Modern School Movement'. Freinet started to use a printing press in the 1920s – at the time a state-of-the-art technology exclusive to the government – for printing texts produced by the rural children under his supervision. In the late 1920s this caused a scandal, yet today it may seem trivial. Facilitated by the wide availability of photocopiers in teachers' staff rooms and printers in the classrooms, every teacher will at some point have stapled loose sheets with students' writing and declared it to be a 'book'.

Such adjusted products – eventually decorated using technical know-how – were never the goal of the Little Books project. In Freinet's approach to pedagogy, designing, producing, publishing and distributing children's own texts are among the most important activities in school, and this implies courage and decision, endurance and diligence on the part of teachers.

Book making is an approach that involves questioning conformity and protectiveness, and stepping into the lifeworlds of children. Here we trace such initiatives back to a specific context, namely the M2 or 'Multi-grade class 2' model of schooling. It takes place in a public primary school in the 15th municipal district of Vienna, Austria, an area with a population that includes a significant number of immigrant minorities. At school enrolment up to 80 per cent of children do not have German as their first language and some speak no German. The school is situated in a 'troublesome' neighbourhood. Various measures are in place to deal with children's superdiversity. One is the school pilot project of 'Viennese modern school multigrade classes' where children aged 6 to 10 are regrouped into the same classroom to learn together, thus allowing the younger children to catch up faster. Other programmes include multilingual alphabetization in various first languages other than German, integrated classes and an 'open school' system that provides after-school care. Here, in addition to overseeing children's extracurricular activity and homework, those taking care of the children do outreach work in the neighbourhood. Thus the Little Books project is set in a school that has numerous alternative pedagogical facilities.

This chapter traces the project's beginnings, looking at several earlier literacy activities. It presents a selection of Little Books that illustrate the broad range of works being produced, focusing on documentaries and fantasy stories, and then examines one particular book, following Busch's work on multilingualism and multimodality (2014). This is followed by a look at the broad sweep of book production, including the production of multilingual books. We conclude with a general description of production processes and editorial policy, and an assessment of the distribution and impact of the Little Books, ranging from internal exchanges at school up to international circulation.[1]

Plapperkiste and Kindernetz

Already by the 1990s children's ideas were given a platform in Schreger's classroom in the form of a multilingual journal called *Die Plapperkiste* ('The Chatter Box'). For two years the magazine was published monthly and distributed across Austria through subscription. It was coloured by hand, over a hundred copies were printed and it was often produced 'secretly', the children quietly returning to school in the afternoons to assist the production. But four years later another cohort of children made it clear that they had no interest in making papers. They were more interested in the computer technology that had replaced the fragile typewriters. In 1997, the *Kindernetz* ('Children's Network'), an interactive website that made free writing for children possible, went online – at that time something of a privilege reserved for large companies that could afford such interactive sites for their employees. Shortly thereafter the 'Digital Diary' was launched. This used the technical possibilities of both the internet and the analogue world: paper copies, but also text, audio, and image or video in digital form (see the M2's project's website, Schreger, 2011a).

These projects are all based on the premise that children's questions and concerns are to be respected and considered an inspiration for schoolwork. Today, multimedia has reached saturation point and the idea of making analogue things appears exciting and attractive to children again. The tactile sensation of the real surpasses the frictionless swiping of the smartphone's glass screen.

5 + 5 + 1 = 1

The M2 multiclass caters for the children's individual needs by offering a multitude of possibilities in an environment that fosters creativity. Following Freinet's approach that schoolwork be similar to real work outside schools, children are in a large part free to pursue their own projects. Using materials laid out at workstations and drawing on a rich classroom library that does not confine itself to schoolbooks, young authors find ample resources for the realization of their projects. The approaches taken by the children can vary, as we see. They usually start by picking up six sheets of paper and announcing that they intend to make a book. Doing so can take anywhere between thirty minutes and three weeks. The critical creative process, however, has long since taken place: idea and execution have come together as a result of previous activities, otherwise no child would undertake the amount of work needed with such persistence. The result is that over five hundred volumes have been produced.

Little Books offer the children a creative framework within which they can express themselves in literary and artistic forms. The books present a low-threshold opportunity to deal with a non-prescribed subject within a defined framework: five pictures + five texts + one cover = a book. To allow the children to direct their attention to the content, they should not be hampered by problems relating to production. The creative and technical aspects are kept separate, but anyone who is interested in the technical aspect of making a book is encouraged to take part in doing so. Every student is given the same opportunity, with neither language, age nor graphic skills as prerequisites – all that is required is an idea that can be realized as a Little Book. However, the imposed limitation on the length of the text is a challenge: how can the story be accommodated within the fixed format of ten pages?

Some books have a single author but many have been produced through the collaboration of children of different backgrounds, adding an important social dimension. A child's special skills are acknowledged and exploited, for example, when word gets out that someone is especially good at drawing cats and cats are required for a story. The respect for this specific skill opens the path for communication.

Over the years, a number of diverse design possibilities have developed, comprising various methods of illustration (drawings, photographs, stamp prints and so on), as well as numerous genres (documentary, reportage, photostories, fantasy stories) – and recently a quiz book emerged. Drawing is the most popular illustration medium, probably because it offers the greatest creative freedom and can be carried out virtually any time and anywhere.

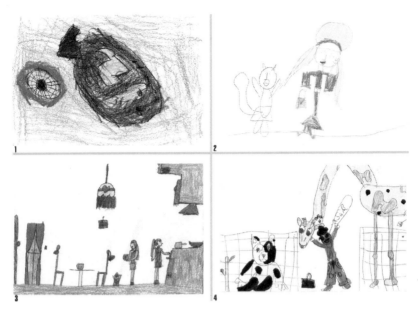

Oskar Kobierski; Nori Wiesmüller; Iqra Ashfaq Ahmad and Ravdip
Guron; Ayshat Gukhaeva

Figure 9.1: (1) Oskar: *Das Zwergenschwimmbad* ('The dwarfs'
swimming pool'), 2013; (2) Nori: *Die Prinzessin und die Stoffkatze 2*
('The princess and the plush cat'), 2009; (3) Iqra and Ravdip: *Das neue
Haus* ('The new house'), 2010; (4) Ayshat: *Tiergarten* ('Zoo'), 2010

Children who feel that their drawing ability is inadequate often collaborate
with children who they consider can draw better or switch to a different
presentation technique: photographs. Photograph books may take the form
of documentaries or photostories that blur boundaries and play with the
attractive aspects inherent to this form of representation (see Figure 9.8,
'*Schöne Kleider*'). In most cases, however, the camera is used for reportage
or documentary purposes.

Documentaries
The authors of the M2 class have recorded numerous events and a wide range
of topics. One of the most compelling formats is the holiday documentary,
which affords a view through somebody else's eyes. When Ravdip returned
from India with a total of 144 photographs on the memory card of the 'kid's
camera' (a camera owned by the M2 class that can be borrowed and taken
home), it was quite a task to review and select the images, and this provoked
many questions and lively discussions. The final book presented a selection
of annotated photographs (see Figure 9.2).

Ravdip Guron

Figure 9.2: Ravdip: *In Indien* ('In India'), 2011

Nemanja's book series about his Serbian home village is another example, completed between November 2006 and March 2008 (Figure 9.3). While the first book shows the houses and streets in plan view and the individual drawings can be put together like a map, in the second volume this changes to a perspective view and the drawings contain many details and depict people. In Volume 3 he uses photographs instead of drawings. Nemanja had by then got hold of a camera and had used it to document his Serbian village. In Volume 4, through the Little Book, we can share in a family gathering on St George's Day – the four volumes are like a slow zooming in, ending at the festival table of the family.

Nemanja Marković

Figure 9.3: Nemanja: Virine Books 1–4, 2006–8

As can be seen here, documentaries can also consist of drawings, and – a common feature of Little Books in general – often use a mixture of different modalities and perspectives. Another distinctive example is Qin-Jie's exclusively hand-drawn documentary describing and illustrating Chinese New Year customs (Figure 9.4). The author is skilled in producing a particular canonical – and very complex – form of character drawings and demonstrates a mastery of Chinese writing.

3: 妈妈给合小孩发红包.

Die Mutter verteilt Geschenkkuverts an die Kinder.

2:小孩子在外面放炮竹.

Kleine Kinder lassen im Freien Raketen steigen.

Qin Jie Yang
Figure 9.4: Qin-Jie: *Neues Jahr* ('New Year'), 2010

Extraordinary events are depicted not only in a far-away homeland, but also in the local classroom. When Neil Kinnock was touring Europe as Chairman of the British Council to promote multilingualism, he heard about the M2 class and visited the school. His encounter was duly documented in a Little Book. The multilingual book – originally written in Serbian and then translated into German – combines children's drawings and photographs made during the visit. One photograph shows Lord Kinnock reading a Little Book (Figure 9.5).

Cover: Naib Makaew; Photograph: Christian Schreger
Figure 9.5: Lord Kinnock at the M2: *Lordbuch* ('Lordbook'), 2007

Fantasy stories

Within the framework of Little Books almost anything is possible. Children are free to explore every subject that matters to them, even when it seems unusual or questionable. It is not surprising that fantasy stories dominate the five hundred volumes of Little Books. They reflect on everything that happens between dream and reality and depict anything – a wish, an event or an idea.

One example is the Little Book *Die Feder, die von alleine schreibt* ('The quill that writes by itself'). Afra first had the idea of making black-and-white pencil drawings. Then she wrote the story about the loneliness of a quill that is no longer used because of computers, even though it can write by itself and just wants to be held in a hand to invent all sorts of texts. Apart from the critical yet poetical stance she takes on writing instruments, her decision to do all the drawings using only pen and pencil is a bold design choice (Figure 9.6).

Afra Graf

Figure 9.6: Afra: *Die Feder, die von alleine schreibt* ('The quill that writes by itself'), 2012

Little Books can be a platform to present oneself, to share one's ideas and to display one's craftsmanship. But they can also fulfil the function of overcoming difficult events in life. Ayshat wrote and illustrated the following book without warning at the end of her first school year. In page after page, the 'forbidden bird' kills one bird after another until all are dead. Ayshat has never commented on her book (Figure 9.7).

Ayshat Gukhaeva

Figure 9.7: Ayshat: *Der verbotene Vogel* ('The forbidden bird'), 2008

Another group of topics springs from the innumerable fantasies children would like to act out. A striking example is the photostory *Schöne Kleider* (Figure 9.8), which enabled its authors to take part in a day trip to London, dressed in their 'best clothes'. Cultural and ethnic differences between the girls from Pakistan, India and Chechnya crumbled instantly given the delight of staging the collectively experienced photostory. The photographs were taken according to exact specifications and sketches were made for the already agreed story. To appear as an actor in their own story in their own book, to play a particular role in their own best clothes and borrowed make-up, gave them immense happiness and this comes through in their book.

Iqra Ashfaq Ahmad; Mata Elbuzdukayeva; Ayshat Gukhaeva; Ravdip
Guron; Iman Gukhaeva

Figure 9.8: Iqra, Mata, Ayshat, Ravdip, Iman: *Schöne Kleider*
('Beautiful clothes'), 2010

Wishes and needs can be wrapped in symbolism and enacted through
animal characters, as Nemanja has done in *Slon I miš* ('The elephant and
the mouse'). It was the first book he wrote, shortly after his arrival in
Vienna, and it tells the story of an elephant that feels like a stranger in
town. Eventually the elephant meets the mouse and they go off to the sea
together (Figure 9.9). The book's symbolic density allows for a thorough
interpretation, spanning multiple layers of signification. It lends itself to a
micro perspective gained by a close reading.

Nemanja Marković

Figure 9.9: Nemanja: *Slon I miš* ('The elephant and the mouse'), 2006

The elephant and the mouse: A story of displacement and friendship

Little Books are a fruitful object of research because we can ask about the author's perspective and how, from a sociolinguistic point of view, they relate to a broader environment. Busch's analysis (2013: 185–91; Busch, 2014) of Nemanja's book is based on a dialogical approach to multimodal text related to Breckner's (2010) method of 'segment analysis'. Theoretical considerations include the relationship of picture and language, and picture and reality, and take into account perception processes, thereby assigning an active role to the beholder. Accordingly, segments are derived from an interplay between the perception process and the picture's formal qualities. They constitute the central element from which a hermeneutical tracing of meaning and its pragmatic context emerges (Breckner, 2010).

Like every Little Book, Nemanja's story is made up of five pages, each containing a visual component – in this case, a drawing – and a short text. Translated into English the text reads:

> One morning the elephant went for a walk (1). On his way he met a mouse (2).
>
> They became friends and decided to go to the seaside (3). When they arrived, the elephant immediately went for a swim and the mouse had a sunbathe (4).
>
> Then the mouse also went for a swim (5).

The text layer can be said to relate a story about becoming friends. However, since meanings can be intertwined and multilayered, especially in a multimodal setting, there are also parallel storylines.

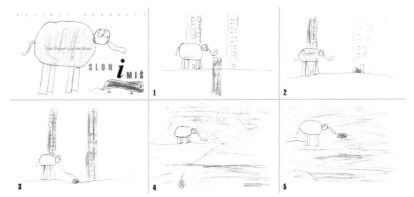

Nemanja Marković
Figure 9.10: The visual layer

Busch judges that:

> the synthesis of different pictorial elements identified in the course of the analysis allows an additional reading of the story: The elephant is out of place, lost in the urban canyon of a big city. He is too big to enter the doors of houses, but small compared to the skyscrapers that reach beyond the rim of the page (1). He perceives (from a safe distance) the town mouse who has the right size for the cityscape and just comes out of a door (2). Elephant and mouse join trunk and tail – they become friends (3). At the seaside, the elephant is in the water, the mouse rests on the beach (4). Then both are in the water, the elephant has brought the mouse into 'his' element (5).
>
> (Busch, 2013: 188)

This interpretation can be traced back to one of the central segments: the elephant, or more specifically, the elephant's head. Figure 9.11 shows that additional information can be obtained from this isolated segment: 'At first the elephant looks straight ahead, his tusks are visible (1). When he meets the mouse (2) he bows down and shows readiness for interaction, the tusks disappear (3), the trunk gains in importance, the mouth becomes more and more visible and smiling (4, 5)' (Busch, 2013: 189).

Original drawing: Nemanja Marković; Editing: Busch/Breckner
Figure 9.11: A segment in focus: the elephant's head

Such close reading of the visual layer ultimately suggests that:

> the author invests the elephant as the main character with emotional expressivity and that he narrates a story of displacement related to his own experience.
>
> (Busch, 2013: 190)

In doing so, the story is also a recourse to already established narrative structures. It is a fairy tale whose protagonists are borrowed from elephant and mouse jokes well known among the children. While it is usually the mouse that plays the leading part, here in Nemanja's story it is the elephant, being 'lost in the city, which is the mouse's environment' (Busch, 2013: 193).

Nemanja Marković
Figure 9.12: A co-presence of multiple voices

As well as the intertextual cues, one can also find multiple voices that went into the final story. Figure 9.12 shows that the written text appears in four versions: Serbian and German, one handwritten and one typed. A closer look reveals that each is a little different:

> In several cases words are not taken from a daily colloquial register but from a more sophisticated one mainly used in written texts. This implies that a dictionary was consulted to work out this first translation. On the other hand certain words indicate in their almost phonological transliteration that they were available for the translation in their vernacular Viennese form (e.g. '*boden*' versus '*baden*'). Apparently Nemanja had some help from outside the classroom. The third and fourth layer are both written by the teacher – bringing the German text into a more conventional form on the one hand, while on the other, immersing himself into a foreign language. Ultimately, typing the text in Serbian implies that he trusts the learner and is prepared to give up control. He is changing his position from being the one who is claiming knowledge to being the one who is learning.
>
> (Busch, 2013: 191)

Such a co-presence of voices also indicates a broader context, namely that of language ideology. The fact that the text is reproduced in hand- and type-written form for both languages, Serbian and German, signals that they are considered equal and that the multivoicedness that went into the production of the book is valued. It becomes a 'heteroglossic text in the Bakhtinian sense as it displays, drawing on different modes of symbolization (written, oral, visual), the interaction of different codes, discourses and voices' (Busch, 2013: 191). The classroom is an important site for identity work and for the discursive negotiation of difference, probably even more so when children are granted such creative freedom. We switch now to a macro perspective on the production of Little Books in the M2 multiclass.

Multilingual books

The multilingual background of many children does not mean that their books are automatically multilingual: this is an option but not an obligation. There are numerous reasons why children choose to write a book in more than one language. Sometimes it might just be an experiment to see how writing multilingually works, but at other times an intimate connection exists with the languages the author uses. The language does not have to be one's first language or some other language perceived as foreign, but might just be one regarded as a 'cool' language to work with. Sometimes it is even cooler to write in German. Some texts have been written in the children's first language and are then translated into German with the support of family members or school colleagues proficient in it. Other books go the opposite way and are translated from German into the respective first, or other, languages. Here the family's support is often significant, because many children master their first language, as spoken at home, orally but not in writing. This is particularly true for Arabic script, used also in Urdu, and the Gurmukhi script used in Punjabi.

The option to write multilingual books is only one possible direction in which the writing process can go. Given that many pupils do not have German as a first language and that their diverse backgrounds consistently receive positive recognition – for example, at one of the weekly cooking sessions in class, attended along with their parents – the fundamental awareness and appreciation of the children's diversity is clear. When asked, children say their multilingualism is an attractive competence and rate their multilingual repertoire as an enhanced means of expression. The caring perspective and the references to a broader context are evidence of a respectful approach to multilingualism that avoids perpetuating stereotypes that draw upon the exotic.

Production process and editorial policy

Since each book is considered essentially as a finished work, the question of orthographic correction is only discussed when the author of the book raises it. Some children present the text in handwritten form, others type it on the computer, and others again dictate it to the teacher or another person. In all three cases, the results are discussed with the author, suggestions are made and errors or ambiguities pointed out. Since the teacher is the first reader and does not know anything about the new book beforehand, quite a few questions can arise at this point. These discussions are extremely important, because it becomes obvious how blind one can be when one does not look closely enough. But just as often, important content does not appear in the text or the images, because the author deemed it to be so obvious that they did not consider it worth mentioning. Thus begins a process we call 'bringing the unspoken language to talk' (Schreger, 2011b: 1).

At this point, one must decide how to deal with the proposed text: should it be left as it is? Is there anything that should be changed? Should an error be corrected? Should the text be rewritten or the proposed version used? Or is the text just supposed to be dictated and set in a suitable typeface for printing? Many children choose to have a corrected version of the self-written text and a printout 'without mistakes'. Other children refuse any corrections because they have invested so much effort into their work already. In any case, handwritten texts are usually accompanied by a typed version, in order to facilitate reading for children who are just starting to learn writing. These encounters at eye level are important.

Images and text are then processed on a computer, whether via scanner, camera or keyboard. They are inserted into simple Word templates that can be edited on any school computer. In the last stage, after the text and illustrations have been arranged on screen, the document is printed by an inkjet colour printer. It has proven useful to use drawing paper for text pages and cardboard for covers. A long-arm stapler is required to staple the A4 sheets. These are then cut with a trimmer, folded and trimmed again at the three edges. Each set of A4 sheets produces two books. The children like to assist with this operation and thereby get an idea of the effort of manual labour. Each author receives a copy of their book and another is placed in the class library. Detailed information on the preparation is available online at the home page of the project (Schreger, 2013).

Distribution and impact of Little Books

Little Books have an audience. They are distributed first of all within the M2 class, then the school, and among peers. Sometimes they are also used in other language classes and in teacher education. Since the project has been awarded various prizes Little Books have also found their way into the media. Although they attract interest outside school, Little Books are a children's medium and fundamentally depend on their authorship. Since 2013 an online video repository of book readings has been established and this is the Little Books distribution channel that first reaches beyond the school context. The project has had a strong impact at school and in the media, locally as well as internationally.

Little Books in teacher education and internationally

Because of the school afternoon programme, children from other classes have come into contact with Little Books. Several children have written books on their own or even signed up for book-making in the M2. Meanwhile, Little Books found their way into scientific literature and serve as a research topic for master's and bachelor's theses (Pernes, 2013). They are also part of teacher education programmes: the University of Teacher Education in Vienna has offered several training courses based on Little Books.

Since 2009/10 the Little Books project has travelled around the world. It has been presented at international conferences, and has found its way from Uppsala in Sweden to Sámi schools in Finland, to a reading club in Cape Town, South Africa, and to Auckland in New Zealand.

Photograph: Brigitta Busch

Figure 9.13: Little Books in Cape Town, South Africa

A number of books were created in Finland and South Africa, based on the templates from the M2 class project. Additionally, some books from the M2 have been translated into English and Xhosa to make them accessible to the children in the Reading Club in Langa, Cape Town.

Little Books Online

Since the beginning of 2013, Little Books have had their own section within the M2 class home page (Schreger, 2013). The children sit on a couch and are filmed while reading, using the camera that is used each day for diary stories in the classroom. They hold a Little Book in their hands while reading, and during post-production the respective text and illustrations are inserted when they turn the pages.

Christian Schreger
Figure 9.14: Screenshot of a book-reading video

Multilingual books are usually read in the original language, the German version being recorded separately, and both recordings are played back with their respective images. Little Books Online is extremely motivating. Clearly, being seated in front of the camera, the pride of being able to read to someone, the pleasure of presenting one's own work, all encourage creativity and the effort of reading aloud, which is often apparent in the video. The children with whom the Little Books project started in 2005 are now 16 or 17 years old, but remarkably, many of these former students are still willing to read their books in front of the camera.

Conclusion

In principle, it is easy to work with projects such as Little Books. But because they can provide an opportunity that appeals to only a certain number of children, it is important to offer a broad range of entry points and complementary activities to what constitutes a publishing ecosystem – and even so, book making might not be for everyone. Such an ecosystem is dynamic and might at any time spawn new kinds of formats, genres and activities. The online video book reading repository is a new component to this assemblage. Naturally, the authors recognize its inherent opportunities and set off to explore them. And by now, after printing a book, children immediately ask when to go and film themselves reading it and, after that, whether it is online. A hallmark of the Little Books project is that it is not dependent on individual techniques but instead offers a range of possibilities that seem to give rise to a matching wealth of ideas. It is an encounter between people and a dialogue between the abilities of everyone involved. And as such it is continually evolving. Such is the experience of making Little Books.

Note

[1] In this chapter we present a number of books, most of which can be found online. The website features authors on film as they read, and thus provides another, and – in a certain sense – more complete representation of the Little Books project. See http://ortnergasse.webonaut.com/m2/kb/ (Schreger, 2013).

References

Breckner, R. (2010) *Sozialtheorie des Bildes: Zur interpretativen Analyse von Bildern und Fotografien*. Bielefeld: Transcript.

Busch, B. (2013) *Mehrsprachigkeit*. Vienna: Facultas.

— (2014) 'Building on heteroglossia and heterogeneity: The experience of a multilingual classroom'. In Blackledge, A. and Creese, A. (eds) *Heteroglossia as Practice and Pedagogy*. New York: Springer, 21–40.

Pernes, S. (2013) 'Die große Freiheit kleiner Bücher: Multimodales Schreiben in der Mehrstufenklasse M2'. Master's thesis, University of Vienna. Online. http://othes.univie.ac.at/27166/ (accessed 22 December 2013).

Schreger, C. (2011a) *Projektseite der M2*. Online. http://ortnergasse.webonaut.com/m2/projekte/ (accessed 22 December 2013).

— (2011b) 'Die "Kleinen Bücher"'. Handout presented at the Department of Linguistics, University of Vienna. Online. http://ortnergasse.webonaut.com/m2/projekte/pdf/kb_kurz.pdf (accessed 22 December 2013).

— (2013) *Kleine Bücher Online*. http://ortnergasse.webonaut.com/m2/kb/ (accessed 22 December 2013).

Index